What the Label
Doesn't Tell You

What the Label Doesn't Tell You

SUE DIBB

Thorsons

An Imprint of HarperCollins*Publishers*

Thorsons
An Imprint of HarperCollins*Publishers*
77–85 Fulham Palace Road,
Hammersmith, London W6 8JB

Published by Thorsons 1997

1 3 5 7 9 10 8 6 4 2

A catalogue record for this book
is available from the British Library

ISBN 0 7225 3497 3

Printed and bound in Great Britain by
Caledonian International Book Manufacturing Ltd, Glasgow

Contents

Acknowledgements   vi
Introduction   vii

Chapter 1   Look at the Label   1
Chapter 2   Added Extras   35
Chapter 3   Shopping for Health   57
Chapter 4   Food for Babies and Children   93
Chapter 5   Slim Hopes   118
Chapter 6   Eat Your Greens   136
Chapter 7   Down on the Farm   163
Chapter 8   Ingene-ious Foods   191

Taking Action   209
Reference Notes   224
Index   229

Acknowledgements

I am indebted to the work of the Food Commission and would like to thank my colleagues, especially Dr Tim Lobstein, for his advice and comments on this book. In addition I would like to thank Dr Mike Rayner, Diane McCrea, Peter Beaumont, Patti Rundall and Dr Erik Millstone for their help and advice and Dan Antal for his encouragement.

I am also grateful to the Consumers' Association and the many other independent researchers and scientists from whose research I have drawn. And finally, a special thank you to the late Caroline Walker, whose campaigning for better food so inspired me.

Introduction

Regular headlines about new genetically-engineered crops, or toxic chemicals in food, leave many people feeling anxious and confused about what's safe to eat. BSE has opened our eyes to some of the less palatable and sometimes scandalous aspects of the way in which our food is produced. But the media move on, and last week's food scare is quickly forgotten. Yet time and time again consumers are left in the dark and unsure about whom to trust.

Surveys show we want more information about the food we eat. Yet often food labels are all we get, and what they tell us is not always useful or easy to understand. And there's much that labels won't tell you at all. This book does exactly what its title says – it reveals what the label *doesn't* tell you, it guides you through the information that you do get, it demystifies the jargon and cuts through the marketing hype.

Obviously it will take more than better food labelling to ensure that we feel confident our food is safe and healthy. It will take a new independent food standards agency which puts consumers' interests first. It means less decisions being taken behind closed doors, and more honesty. We're quite capable of making up our own minds once we've been given the facts – facts we can trust – not the partial truth of advertising slogans or government ministers, covering up years of incompetence and collusion.

A growing interest in exactly what food contains, how it has been produced and what effect it has on our health and on the environment has contributed to pressure for change. More and more people are prepared to seek out food that is produced without pesticides, growth-promoters and other chemicals – food that is produced with less damage to the environment, which is kinder to animals and which is healthier, too. Whatever you like to eat, this book gives you the crucial facts to help you make your own choices.

Look at the Label

How can you tell the difference between one food and another when you're trying to judge which to buy? When we mainly bought raw, unwrapped ingredients we used to rely on our senses – we'd know whether fruit was ripe by giving it a squeeze, and we'd judge how fresh it was by its colour or its smell. But these days we are buying many more foods that have been processed in one way or another and have so much packaging and wrapping it's often impossible even to *see* the food, let alone smell or feel it.

We have many ways of choosing what we buy. Cost is often important, as are taste, convenience and health, but so is attractive packaging and advertising. Whether we are conscious of it or not, the packaging of a product can make it more appealing, especially for kids. We've all got favourite foods that we buy time and time again, though it's likely that we're sometimes tempted to try products promising 'new improved flavours' or offering to make us healthier. The brightly coloured flash on the front of the pack tempts us to pop it in the trolley, but can we be sure about what we're really getting?

To find out what we are buying it's now down to us to take a close look at the label. It should be simple to find out what the food is made of, whether it's good for us and safe to eat. Good labels can be a big help in making healthy food choices. But it's not always so simple. Some foods and drinks don't have to tell you what's in them at all. And you can be kept in the dark about a whole host of other information, such as the way food has been produced, treated and processed. Even when food *is* labelled, the information given is often neither clear nor complete.

What's in a Name?

A product's name is the first guide to what you're buying. The law says that the name of a food must not be misleading. But it's still easy to be confused. Don't assume that a product's name is a full guide to what it contains. For example, you could be forgiven for thinking that there is strawberry in a strawberry *flavour* milkshake. But there isn't. And there needn't be a hint of real cheese and onion in cheese and onion *flavour* crisps, or any real beef and tomato in beef and tomato *flavour* pot noodles – just artificial flavours from the laboratory.

Flavoured (with an *-ed*) is another matter. The flavouring in a strawberry-*flavoured* drink must come completely or mainly from real strawberries – though you still might not get very much. In 1991 the Government's expert advisory committee said it would be much less confusing if the word 'flavour' were replaced by 'taste' – but this recommendation has never been implemented by the manufacturers.

The name should also say if a food has been processed in any way – UHT milk, for example, or smoked salmon. However, if the food has been made from genetically-modified ingredients you won't necessarily find anything on the label to tell you so, nor if it has been treated with pesticides after harvesting.

Some foods have 'prescribed' names, which means they must meet strict criteria for their ingredients. For example, to be called margarine a spread must contain at least 80 per cent fat. But for too many foods there are no such standards and it is very difficult, if not impossible, to know what you are buying. For example, no one expects cream crackers to contain cream, but you'd expect a reasonable amount of meat in a sausage roll, and a decent amount of fish in a fish cake. You'd expect it, but will you get it? Well you may or may not, depending on the product.

Many foods used to have to conform to quality or composition standards, but some of these were removed in 1984 and there are plans for more to go. For example, fish cakes no longer need to contain at least 35 per cent fish, and cooked ham can be pumped full of additives and ingredients as long as they are declared in the ingredients list or in the product name. (*See 'Hamming it Up', page 10.*)

So, is it simply a matter of checking the labels? Ah, no, that would be too easy. With a few exceptions, food companies are *not* obliged to tell you how much of an ingredient is in a food. So, for example, you can't actually tell how much fish is in a fish finger – although in many cases fish makes up less than half the product – or how much fruit juice in a juice drink – although it may be as little as 5 per cent.

We might get some idea of the relative amount of an ingredient from its placing on the ingredients list (the heaviest ingredients must come first). But there's no real way we can compare different products for quality or value for money unless the manufacturer volunteers to tell us how much of each ingredient is in their product. As you can imagine, it's more likely to be manufacturers of better quality products who volunteer this information, rather than those who skimp on more expensive ingredients. For many years now we've been promised QUID – quantitative ingredient declarations – where manufacturers would be obliged to disclose how much of an ingredient is in a product. Some day this will become law, even so its scope has been narrowed and it is only likely to apply to a limited number of ingredients – the ones which feature in a product's name or description.

Lifting the Lid

How can you tell how much actual fruit you're getting when you buy a tin of fruit? You can't. As little as 56 per cent of the declared net weight could be fruit – compared with the syrup or fruit juice that it comes in – and that's only an industry guideline, not the law. It's the same for other tinned foods. One survey[1] found up to 29 per cent of the weight of tinned tuna was actually oil (up to 35 per cent is allowed by law) – twice the amount of oil found in the best brands. The only way you could compare brands on a value-for-money basis is if their drained weights were declared – but that's not covered by law.

Up in Smoke

Has smoked bacon really been smoked? Not necessarily. It's more likely to be the result of adding 'smoke flavour' as a liquid solution. Even then there's a choice between 'natural gaseous smoke' (concentrated into a liquid) or synthetic flavouring agents. Bacon made this way has up to 10 per cent more water than bacon made the traditional way, which is one reason modern bacon bubbles and froths, rather than sizzles, in the frying pan.

What Labels Must Tell You by Law

- **Weight**. Most foods declare a weight or volume, though there are exceptions – such as foods sold by quantity (e.g. six jam tarts). The big e often found on packets means that the average weight must be accurate, but the weight of each pack may vary slightly.
- **Datemarking**. Most packaged food has to carry a datemark as an important safeguard against food which may be unfit to eat – or just past its best. **Use by dates** are for highly perishable foods such as some meat products or ready-prepared foods. Keeping food beyond its 'use by' date could be a health risk. Foods which can safely be kept for longer, e.g. tinned or packet foods, carry a **best before** date. It doesn't mean that the food will be dangerous beyond that

date, just that it may then no longer be at its best. Both kinds of datemarking assume you follow the storage instructions correctly. Foods which are intended to be eaten quickly, such as fresh fruit and vegetables and bread, may not carry a datemark at all.

- **Ingredients list**. Ingredients, including additives, must be listed in descending order of weight (so the heaviest is listed first, the lightest last). It should include all ingredients, but there are some exceptions – including water if it makes up less than 5 per cent of the product, and some additives used in processing. In addition, flavouring additives don't have to be declared individually. Some products, such as alcoholic drinks, are also excluded from having to declare their ingredients (*see 'Missing Ingredients, page 6*). Ingredients lists don't have to tell you how much of an ingredient is in the food, although the rules governing this may change in coming years. Exceptions are the meat content of a meat product, which must be declared (as in 'contains a minimum of 60% meat'), or if a food comes with an 'extra' claim – such as 'extra jam' or 'extra chocolate' – in which case the label must show the minimum amount of that ingredient.
- **Manufacturer's name and address**. The name and address of the maker, packer or retailer must appear, so you can contact them if you want. (*See Appendix: Taking Action.*)
- **Place of origin**. Must be given if there is a chance the consumer could be misled on this point.
- **Nutrition information**. Must be given if a claim is made on the packaging about the product's nutritional value e.g. low fat or high fibre.

Checking Out the Ingredients

When buying foods it's possible to compare prices, but trying to judge quality, particularly of processed foods, is often much harder. Don't assume that because an ingredient features in the name of a product that there's a lot of it in there. The product can contain larger amounts of other ingredients.

To compare products, check the placing of important ingredients in the ingredients list. For example, if two orange juice drinks cost about the same, but one has 'water' as its first ingredient and the other has 'orange juice', you'll know you'll be getting more juice for your money with the second one. Similarly, a strawberry yoghurt that lists sugar higher than strawberries probably has only a small amount of fruit in it, no matter how pink it looks.

But ingredients-list checking is not foolproof. Fat and sugar may be added in many guises (*see 'Hidden Ingredients', page 10*); added air, as in foods like ice cream, doesn't count at all.

Missing Ingredients

You'd expect all ingredients to be listed, but not all need be, and some foods don't have to declare what's in them at all.

- **Unwrapped foods**. Food that is sold unwrapped, such as some breads, food from a cooked food counter or delicatessen counter and some sweets, doesn't have to carry a full ingredients list. A ticket or notice nearby should by law show its proper name and the type of any main additives in it (e.g. 'contains preservative').
- **Restaurant and take-away foods.** There's no requirement to list any of the ingredients in these kinds of foods. For some people this could be a matter of life and death. In 1995 four people died as a result of allergic reactions to nuts in foods bought from restaurants and take-aways.
- **Alcoholic drinks** don't have to declare their ingredients. There's no good reason why they shouldn't, except that brewers and wine-makers are reluctant to let us know what additives and other unexpected ingredients might be in their products. For some people, particularly those people who are sensitive to sulphites (commonly used as preservatives in wine), this lack of labelling can be a health hazard. On the other hand, low-alcohol drinks must declare their ingredients. There are plans for all alcoholic drinks to be properly

labelled, but it's likely to be a long time before an agreement is reached with the drinks companies about this.

- **Additives.** Most additives have to be declared in ingredients lists, but not all. There are several thousand **flavouring additives**, but as they don't have E numbers they don't have to be listed individually. In addition, **processing aids** do not have to be declared even though traces may carry over into the final product. These additives include enzymes to change the nature of the food, propellants and solvents to carry additives into the food, and oils used to grease machinery and baking trays.

- **Irradiated ingredients.** Any food or ingredient that has been irradiated must be labelled as such – that is, unless it makes up less than 25 per cent of a compound ingredient. For example, if the black pepper in salami used in a pizza has been irradiated, you won't find anything on the label to tell you – and this is quite legal.

- **Quantity of ingredients.** With some exceptions (such as most meat products), manufacturers don't have to declare how much of each ingredient is in their product.

- **Meat content.** Most meat products should declare how much meat is in them. But some foods such as soup and baby foods are exempt. A loophole in the regulations means that soup – both canned and packet – can have as little meat as it likes and still call itself a meat soup. One survey[2] found some chicken soups with virtually no chicken meat, and others with more salt and monosodium glutamate than chicken.

Missing Information

It's not just ingredients that may be missing from the label. Other key information that would tell us about the nutritional quality of the food, about the way it was produced and whether it contains genetically-engineered ingredients may be completely absent. Even information about the country of origin may not be straightforward.

- **Nutrition information** – With certain exceptions there's no obligation on manufacturers to tell us anything about the nutritional quality of a food – for example how much fat or sugar it contains. And even when they do provide some information it's often lacking in detail or too confusingly presented to be much use in helping shoppers to make healthier choices (*see 'Making Sense of Nutrition Labelling', page 72*).

- **Production methods** – Shoppers say they want more information about the way their food is produced and processed, but all too often this information is lacking. You won't find on the label any information about pesticides, fertilisers, growth hormones or antibiotics used to produce a food, even though residues of these chemicals may remain in the food. Only the Co-op label their battery eggs as 'intensively produced' – no other manufacturer declares this. And most foods containing genetically-altered ingredients won't have to mention the fact on the label (*see 'Ingene-ious Foods', page 191*).

- **Country of origin** – You would think that details of the country of origin of a food would be straightforward. But that's not always so. The place or origin of a food does not necessarily mean the country in which the food was grown – it can be used to mean the country in which the food last underwent a 'substantial change'. So don't assume that all olive oil labelled as 'produced in Italy' or 'made in Italy' – and sold at the best prices – comes from Italian olives. Spanish, Greek or North African olives can be pressed and the oil bottled in Italy – and the oil called Italian olive oil. Labelling laws don't require country of origin labels on imported meat, and in any case labels can be ambiguous. It may be marked with the initials of an EU country, e.g. UK, but this might not be its country of origin. It's a health mark which shows where the meat was cut or packed, rather than reared. And meat cut in butchers is exempt.

When the Nutrition Information Doesn't Add Up

When companies do provide nutritional information we assume that the figures given are correct. But not always so, according to the Consumers' Association. Their survey[3] of over 70 packets, tubs and tins of food found that nearly half the figures for calories, fat, fibre, sodium, etc. were wrong by more than 10 per cent.

Hamming It Up

The label may say 'ham', but you'll need to read the small print to judge the quality of what you are buying.

Ham or **shoulder** should mean the traditional product: cured meat from the hind leg of a pig, either on or off the bone.

Ham (or shoulder) formed from cuts of legs means the product looks like a cut, joint or slice of meat but has been made up of pieces of meat from more than one leg (or shoulder).

Reformed ham is similar to the above but also contains fine fragments of meat and/or meat emulsion.

Added extras: Ham can contain a range of added ingredients and additives that you might not expect, including gelatin, sugars, nitrite preservatives, phosphates and gums, which help hold in water, salt, flavourings, meat substitutes such as milk and soya proteins, and water. In fact, manufacturers can add as much water as they like – some hams can be over 25 per cent water. The amount of added water should be declared on the label (though the first 5 per cent is exempt), but if meat substitutes such as soya, starch and milk protein (casein) are also used, the label doesn't have to say how much water there is – just 'with added water'.

Hidden Ingredients

It's not always easy to spot ingredients you may wish to check out or avoid.

HIDDEN SUGARS

There are different ways in which manufacturers can disguise the word 'sugar'. Sucrose is just another name for refined sugar, but there is also glucose, fructose, dextrose – in fact, any ingredient that ends in -ose is a type of sugar. Then there is glucose syrup, honey and fruit juices – all of which are used to sweeten food and which are just as bad for teeth (*see Chapter 3*).

A product may contain different types of sugar – a breakfast cereal, for example, may list three different types of added sugar – brown sugar, sugar, and honey. By listing each type of sugar separately, each appears lower down the ingredients list – making it harder from the ingredients list to judge how much sugar is in the cereal overall.

And you may find that manufacturers keep the amount of sugar in their products secret. Many manufacturers of sweet foods, including soft drinks – if they provide any nutrition information at all – declare only a carbohydrate figure, and fail to say that most or all of the carbohydrates in the drink are sugars – quite legally.

HIDDEN FATS

Fat, too, can come in many disguises. Here are some of them: margarine, hydrogenated vegetable oil, butter, lard, oils, animal fat, mono-, di- or triglycerides.

HIDDEN PEANUTS

One in 200 people suffers an allergy to peanuts. Of these, one-third experience severe symptoms including anaphylactic shock, which can be fatal. Even minute amounts can trigger adverse reactions in sensitive individuals. Campaigns for better labelling were started after the tragic death of one young girl who unwittingly ate peanuts in a lemon meringue bought in a department store restaurant.

It can be hard to detect whether foods contain peanuts. Check ingredients lists of foods such as biscuits, cakes, breakfast cereals, confectionery and savoury snacks. Peanut oil (also known as groundnut oil), for example, can turn up in quite unexpected places, even in children's lollies – but most likely it will only be listed as vegetable oil. Some manufacturers now put warning labels on foods that contain peanuts or peanut ingredients, but even this may not be enough as cross-contamination during food processing can transfer minute amounts. It's even harder when eating out, as there are generally no labels.

Less well known is allergy to sesame, which estimates suggest affect one in 2,000. Sesame is found in hummus, veggie burgers, rice cakes, burger baps, bagels and many Oriental foods. (*See 'Allergies', page 116.*)

HIDDEN BEEF

With concerns about BSE (*see page 181*) many people are wary of beef. It's easy to walk along supermarket shelves and avoid the meat clearly labelled 'beef' or 'steak', but it's much less easy to avoid the hidden beef ingredients or beef derivatives that can turn up, often quite unexpectedly in foods such as chicken gravy granules, chicken stew with dumplings, salami, stuffing mixes, ready meals, pasties, biscuits and even Christmas pudding. Perhaps even more worrying for some parents is the hidden beef in baby foods. Many non-beef sounding savoury baby foods may contain 'meat extract', beef bouillon, beef stock or gelatin.

Watch Out For

- **beef fat** or the non-specific **animal fat**. 'Animal fat' may be lard (pig fat), tallow or suet (both beef fats).
- **stock or bone stock.**

- **meat or beef extract**. 'Meat extract' is an ambiguous term – manufacturers may change the sources frequently, or the extract may be made from a multi-species blend.
- **gelatin**. 'Gelatin', used in many sweets, desserts and other foods, is made from pigskin, cattle hides or bones. Processing is known to reduce the infectiousness of the BSE agent, and as an added precaution only imported bovine raw material can be used in its production.
- **'Composite ingredients'** can be poorly defined. For example, a tin of beans with sausages may only list 'sausages' as an ingredient and say nothing about the meat included.

New labelling rules now prohibit the catch-all phrase 'meat' from food labels – and phrases such as 'other meats', 'meat stock' and 'mechanically recovered meat' will have to declare the species. But that still leaves animal fat – manufacturers don't have to tell you where it has come from.

Mmm, MRM

Mechanically recovered meat (MRM) is an ingredient which was until recently impossible to identify – it simply wasn't labelled. MRM is the carcass scrapings removed from bones once the best meat has already been removed. The remaining bits are put through a machine, similar to a giant washing machine, which strips every last shred of tissue from the bones. This makes a watery, greasy paste, potentially full of bacteria, which is coloured with additives to make it look pink and often added to pies, sausages and patés. Not surprisingly, manufacturers were cagey about declaring its presence.

It took the Government six years, after it banned cattle vertebrae in food for human consumption, to ban MRM made from the scrapings from cattle vertebrae – potentially one of the more BSE-infective parts of the carcass. In making the announcement of its ban, the then Agriculture Minister Douglas Hogg said that he was pleased to be acting 'promptly'.

Consumer groups argued long and hard that food labels should declare the presence of MRM, on the grounds that it is sufficiently different from what most people expect by the word 'meat'. Now that consumer pressure has forced the European Commission to say that all MRM should be labelled, we have been given the right to know what's in our food and are better able to judge the quality of what we are buying.

HIDDEN GENETICALLY-ENGINEERED INGREDIENTS

Genetically-modified soya and maize (corn) are being imported into the European Union, raising the possibility that in future many common foods will contain genetically-engineered ingredients with nothing on the label to tell you (*see Chapter 8*).

Hidden Soya Ingredients

An estimated 60 per cent of the processed food we eat contains soya in one form or another. In addition to the soya ingredients listed on labels, soya may find its way into foods that are not so easy to check up on.

- **Vegetable protein, hydrolysed vegetable protein and protein isolate**: found in sausages and other meat products, gravy powder, soups, stock cubes, coffee creamers, frozen desserts and in the brine injected in cured meats such as ham and bacon.
- **Textured vegetable protein**: in meat products, meat substitutes and vegetarian foods.
- **Lecithin**: an emulsifier used in a wide range of foods including chocolate, margarine, breakfast cereals, bread, cakes and biscuits.
- **Vegetable oil, vegetable fat, hydrogenated vegetable oil**: in many foods including cakes and biscuits, margarines, crisps, fried foods, fast foods such as French fries and take-aways.
- **Unlabelled soya flour**: in bread and baked products bought unwrapped.

Hidden Maize Ingredients

- **Maize flour:** used for breakfast cereals, snack foods, bakery products and brewing.
- **Maize oil:** used in margarines and frying and salad dressing oils.
- **Modified starch and glucose syrup:** used in processed foods, confectionery and soft drinks.

HIDDEN ANIMAL PRODUCTS

Vegetarians and vegans need to read labels carefully to avoid hidden animal products, though in some cases this won't be possible, as the ingredients won't be declared on the label.

- **Animal fat**: can be found in biscuits, cakes and pastries.
- **Fish oils**: now added as a health ingredient to many foods.
- **Rennet**: traditionally used in cheese-making, made from calves' stomachs – as a 'processing aid', it isn't listed on ingredients lists.
- **Gelatin**: many foods, including yoghurts, jellies and sweets may contain gelatin. It is increasingly used in low-fat dairy products and spreads.
- **Whey, lactose, casein and caseinates**: derived from milk.
- **Eggs**: watch out for constituents of eggs such as albumen, lecithin and emulsifier.
- **Fruit**: much fruit, particularly apples and citrus fruit, is often waxed with shellac – an insect secretion – and beeswax. Not labelled.
- **Honey**: produced by bees.
- **Beers and wines**: 'finings' for clarifying drinks may be derived from milk, eggs, fish or mineral earths and seaweed, but you won't find anything on the label to tell you.
- **Cochineal**: natural colouring made from crushed female Mexican cactus beetles.
- **Mono- and di-glycerides of fatty acids**: emulsifier additives which may be derived from animal sources.

HIDDEN GLUTEN

People with coeliac disease are unable to tolerate gluten, the protein found in wheat, barley, oats and rye, as it damages the lining of their small intestine. This condition needs medical diagnosis and advice on diet. This is not the same as an allergy or intolerance to wheat, which affects some people, although some of the foods such people are advised to avoid may be similar. However, many specially formulated 'gluten-free' foods contain wheat starch and are therefore not suitable for people with wheat intolerance.

Watch Out For

- breads, biscuits, cakes, puddings, breakfast cereals, ready mixes and many processed foods;
- ingredients such as binders, fillers, starch, cereal starch, modified starch, cereal protein which may contain gluten;
- gluten in foods for babies under six months (*see 'Baby Foods', page 109*).

HIDDEN DAIRY PRODUCTS

Milk and milk products are among the most common triggers of food allergies and intolerance. There are two causes: some people react to the protein in cow's milk (casein), while others are affected by milk sugar (lactose). Care should be taken with introducing dairy products to babies (*see 'Follow-on milks', page 108*).

Watch Out For

- casein, caseinate, lactose and whey;
- lactose used as a filler in some food supplements, sweeteners and monosodium glutamate seasonings.

What's in a Name? – Bottled Water

Spring water conjures up an image of purity and health – rather like **mineral water**, you might think. But you'd be wrong. There's a world of difference between mineral water and spring water. Mineral water has been a huge success and it's a class product. You can't just bottle stuff from a hole in the ground. 'Natural mineral water' is a name protected by law. The water has to come from an officially recognised source, registered and approved, with the water meeting a range of purity standards and its label declaring details of the mineral analysis.

But spring water has no such restrictions. All bottled water must comply with drinking water purity regulations, but there's no legal definition of 'spring' – it could just come from a tap. Some manufacturers have agreed that 'spring' water should have come from a single underground source, but it can have undergone a range of treatments including blending, filtration and ultra-violet treatment.

Flavoured spring water more often than not includes chemical additives such as artificial sweeteners, preservatives (including E211 sodium benzoate, which has been linked to hyperactivity, asthma and skin rashes), colours and flavourings. If you are lucky there might be a small amount of fruit juice or some 'natural fruit flavours', but you might also get several teaspoons of sugar in the bottle. Don't be fooled – they are soft drinks dressed up to look healthy and high class – often with a price to match!

What's in a Name? – Bread

White – we still buy more white bread than any other type. It's made with white flour which has had all the bran and wheatgerm of the wheat grain removed, and hence many of its nutrients (although some vitamins and minerals must be added back by law). It can either be chemically whitened – bleached – or unbleached. Added-fibre white breads have softened grains added.

Brown – Brown bread may still retain some of the bran and wheatgerm, but it can be little more than dyed white bread –

caramel is the most common colouring used to add colour. **Granary** is a type of brown bread which is a registered trademark for Rank Hovis Ltd and which they use for their 'Original and Authentic Malted Brown Bread'.

Wholemeal – by law wholemeal bread must be made with 100 per cent wholemeal flour which includes the whole of the wheat or other grain. It's more naturally nutritious than white or brown bread as it retains vitamins, minerals and fibre which are lost during the milling of white flour.

What's in a Name? – Chocolate

For years one of the fiercest debates in Europe has not been about the Maastricht Treaty or the Single European Currency. It's been about chocolate. For over 20 years, bureaucrats and businessmen have been locked into one of the longest-running Euro-disputes. The problem is British chocolate, which causes some countries, including Belgium and France, to throw up their hands in horror. For years most big British chocolate manufacturers have been quite legally adding vegetable fat along with the cocoa butter. That's adulteration, say many of our European partners. Chocolate must be made with pure cocoa butter, they demand – your inferior stuff should be called 'vegolate'. Some countries even banned British chocolate from their shelves. At last, a compromise seemed to be reached – chocolate would be allowed to contain up to 5 per cent vegetable fat – but with eight European countries still demanding strict purity standards, this one could run and run ...

Where's the Beef?

Do you know what you're getting when you buy a meat product? To most of us, meat is the fleshy muscle part of the animal, but the law says that 'meat' can mean not only the flesh, but also the fat, skin, rind, gristle and sinew 'in amounts normally associated with the flesh used'. This vague definition makes it difficult for food law enforcement officers to challenge manufacturers whom they think have used too much of the cheaper parts of the animal and not enough of the expensive muscle.

Lean meat – With many of us looking for healthier cuts of meat, 'lean' or 'extra lean' meat seems a good bet. But there is no legal definition of 'lean' or 'extra lean'. It's best to check the nutrition panel – if there is one – to see exactly how much fat is in the meat. Raw meat doesn't always come with such information.

One thing you can be sure of is that you'll be paying more for 'trimmed' or 'lean' meat. Trimmed meat is no different from any other meat – it's just had the visible fat trimmed off. You could do that yourself, but if the supermarket does it for you, you could be paying considerably more. The Consumers' Association have found you could save 50 per cent of the cost by trimming the meat yourself.

Sausage Secrets

We treat the British banger as part of our heritage. Indeed, Government ministers boldly battled with their European counterparts to save it for the nation, though the truth is a little less heroic. Europe wanted to ban the artificial colouring red 2G (E128) which was already banned in many other European countries due to questions over its safety. But the British Government, on behalf of sausage makers, won the right for the manufacturers to continue to use it to dye fat and mechanically recovered meat red so that it looks like lean meat.

Like many meat products, sausages must conform to minimum standards. Pork sausages must contain a minimum of 65 per cent meat, others can have as little as 50 per cent. But what passes as 'meat'? As described above, meat can include fat and the skin, rind, gristle and sinew. Half the 'meat' must be 'lean meat', but 10 per cent of even this 'lean meat' can be fat, and a further 10 per cent gristle; half the regular 'meat' can be fat and gristle.

Typically, sausages are around 20 per cent fat by weight. But the fattiest sausages can have a 'meat' content that is half fat – making a

---

third of the whole sausage fat. Extra gristle in the form of rind is also a traditional sausage ingredient, as is mechanically recovered meat. And if you're expecting only pork meat in a pork sausage, you could be in for a surprise. Up to a fifth need not even be pork. And only half the 'meat content' of a beef sausage actually has to be beef.

Low-fat sausages may have less fat than regular ones, but that still doesn't make them a low-fat food.

Premium sausages – If the label says premium, you'd expect to get a better quality product for your money. But don't count on it. The word premium has no legal definition. You may get more lean meat if you buy 'premium' pork sausages, but it's not guaranteed. One survey[4] found that premium sausages tended to be fattier, to have no more lean meat, and to give poorer value for money compared with regular sausages. But you can count on paying more for them.

MEAT RULES FACE THE CHOP

If Government deregulation proposals get the go-ahead, quality standards for meat products such as sausages, burgers, corned beef and luncheon meat could be swept away. At present these meat products must contain a minimum amount of meat, but under new proposals manufacturers will be able to put in as little meat as they wish as long as they declare the meat content somewhere on the packet. Back in the 1980s when quality standards were abolished for other meat products such as pies and pasties, the amount of meat in many products fell dramatically.

Give Us a Squeeze

Confused by juice labels? Take orange juice – you can choose from 'freshly squeezed', 'pure', 'concentrated', 'premium', 'juice drinks', 'short-life', 'long life' – the choice is yours. But do you know what you are buying?

Take the most popular juice – orange. Typically oranges are picked and squeezed and the juice concentrated, frozen and shipped to the UK. Here water is re-added, the juice is heat-treated and packed – that's your standard **long life 'pure' juice.** Other **'made from concentrate'** juices may have less severe heat treatment and thus a shorter shelf-life.

Freshly squeezed juice – oranges are shipped to the UK where they may be stored under refrigeration for several months. After squeezing, juice is kept chilled rather than heat-treated – unless it's going to be sold as pasteurised – and delivered to retailers within 24 hours. Freshly squeezed juices are more expensive but usually score more highly in taste tests. They also typically have more vitamin C – up to twice as much as long-life orange juice.

Premium juices are a mixture, usually half and half, of concentrate and freshly squeezed juice.

Pure squeezed or **Florida squeezed** juice is pressed abroad, the juice pasteurised, possibly frozen and shipped without being concentrated.

Pure, unsweetened juices should contain no added sugars except the 15 g per litre which manufacturers are allowed to add undeclared to 'adjust' for variations in the sweetness of different types of oranges. But Government tests in 1991 found that two-thirds of the 21 brands of 'unsweetened' orange juice tested contained added sugar above the legally permitted limit. Half also contained extra water – added in the form of pulpwash, which is produced by soaking already squeezed oranges in water and then giving them another squeeze. Ten out of 17 samples had fruit acids added to disguise the taste of the added sugar and water.

Sweetened juices can contain between 15 and 100 g per litre added sugar, but this must be declared on the label.

Juice drinks are often sold to look like pure juice, with pictures of fruit on the front and a price to match. While a manufacturer of 'pure' juice can be prosecuted for adding sugar and water, if they call it a 'drink' it's quite legal. Some juice drinks contain as little as 5 to 10 per cent – juice – yet there doesn't have to be anything on the label to say so. Some may have more added sugar than juice, while others can come with a cocktail of added flavourings, colours and artificial sweeteners.

Diabetic Labels

People with diabetes need to be more careful than most when it comes to the food they eat. Yet many foods claiming to be suitable for people with diabetes have been found to break labelling laws. In 1995 Cheshire Trading Standards officers found 16 out of 23 failed to comply with the rules forbidding a product to call itself 'diabetic' if in fact it has more calories or fat than conventional equivalents.[5] The British Diabetic Association says the claim 'diabetic' is misleading. Some other countries do not allow the claim at all.

Alcoholic Haze

Are you confused when searching for a suitable drink for drivers? You'll see brews labelled 'reduced alcohol', 'low alcohol', 'de-alcoholised' and 'alcohol-free' as well as the meaningless 'light' – in some cases this doesn't refer to alcohol at all, just to the colour. What's even more confusing is that some 'low alcohol' products have more alcohol than other full-strength products. Even alcohol-free drinks can contain some alcohol.

If this weren't confusing enough, every other European country has completely different definitions, which is making European agreement a bit of a nightmare. Before making your choice it's wise to ignore the claims and take a close look at the actual amount of alcohol each product contains.

Microwave Labelling

In 1992 new labelling for microwave ovens and food packs was introduced to help ensure that foods would be properly cooked and reheated in microwave ovens. This followed the results of Government research which found that one in three microwave ovens failed to heat food adequately. If that weren't bad enough, the Ministry of Agriculture, Fisheries and Food (MAFF) caused a furore by refusing to name the models which had failed the test, although they had passed the results on to the manufacturers.

The labels on the ovens tell you the power of the oven in watts (e.g. 800W) and its heating category (a letter from A to E). Foods that are suitable for microwaving are marked with the microwave symbol and include instructions for heating the food depending on the power of the oven. Sounds complicated? Microwaves were designed to make our lives easier, but it is *very* important to follow all the cooking instructions, including standing time and stirring, and to check that the food really is piping hot all the way through before you eat it.

Countering the Claims

Not many of us have the time or inclination to scour the small print of every product that we buy – certainly not on a busy Saturday morning in the local supermarket with the kids in tow. Manufacturers know this; they also know that busy shoppers are much more likely to be attracted to the big print on the front of the packet – the claims and the images that lead us to believe that we are buying a wholesome and healthy food. Words like 'farmhouse', 'traditional' and 'natural' all conjure up cosy images of homemade food which is usually a far cry from the factory in which it was really made.

NATURAL

Natural is a real buzz word – it conjures up the image of the kind of food we'd really like – food that is wholesome, nutritious and free from any hidden nasties. But it's a much misused word – phrases like 'full of natural goodness', 'naturally better' and 'natural choice' are actually meaningless and are likely to mislead us. Manufacturers should follow guidelines and only use 'natural' to describe single foods to which nothing has been added and which has received only simple processing such as freezing, pasteurisation or traditional baking – but these are only guidelines, not law.

When it comes to additives and flavourings, they can only be described as natural if they are not synthetically made. But just to confuse matters, some can be described as nature-identical. That means they've still been made in a laboratory, rather than from natural ingredients, but are chemically the same. 'Natural' can also include colours found in tree bark (annatto), burnt vegetables (carbon black), insects (cochineal) and flamingo feathers (canthaxanthin) – not substances that we normally associate with food.

And we should perhaps remember that not everything natural is quite so benign. Foods can naturally contain toxins. For example, beans such as red kidneys need to be cooked thoroughly to destroy their toxins, which would otherwise cause stomach aches. We should also avoid green parts of potatoes. Nuts which are not stored properly can develop a poisonous mould known as aflatoxin, although regulations should keep the amounts at safe levels.

'Traditional', 'farmhouse', 'original', 'special', 'selected', 'healthy', 'wholesome' – these are just some of the myriad words that help to persuade us that we are buying something that is of superior quality, that is better for us or that is made in an old-fashioned way that reassures us about its origins. But without any further explanation all these words are meaningless, so don't place too much weight on these kinds of claims.

Style – this little word is used to hide a multitude of sins. What it really means is that it's not the real thing – that it is some kind of imitation, which, more often than not, is a far cry from the original product. Greek-style yoghurt, for example, is not the same as traditional Greek yoghurt.

Fresh – we like to think that our food is fresh – freshly harvested, freshly baked, freshly-squeezed or freshly laid, but are we being misled? Not all 'fresh' food is as fresh as you might think.

How Fresh Is Fresh?

It may look fresh, but is it? As the chain from farm to supermarket becomes longer, technologists are developing ways in which our food can be kept looking fresh for longer. Whether it's 'fresh' ready meals, soups and pasta in the chilled cabinet, fresh meat and fish

---

or fresh fruit and vegetables, fresh is what we are increasingly demanding. But most fresh food doesn't stay 'fresh' for very long, so how do supermarkets manage to keep it looking that way?

Wax and Shine

Much modern fruit comes not only blemish-free, uniformly-sized and air-freighted halfway round the world, but there's a fair chance it also comes treated with a waxy coating to enhance its appearance and to extend shelf-life.

The wax itself is cosmetic and may be harmless, though if you're a vegan you might want to avoid shellac – an insect secretion – and beeswax. But there's often an added extra – fungicides, used to prevent fruit going bad during storage. Waxes can seal these pesticides into food and make them almost impossible to wash off.

Unlike the US, retailers don't need to tell you if fruit is waxed, though some supermarkets sell unwaxed fruit such as oranges and lemons. In the US a sign must read *'coated with food-grade animal-based wax, vegetable-, petroleum-, beeswax-, and/or shellac-based wax or resin, to maintain freshness'* as appropriate – yum, yum.

Modified Atmosphere Packaging

One of the best-kept secrets of freshness is modified atmosphere packaging. Much fresh meat, fish, salads, fresh herbs and other foods such as fresh pasta come sealed in modified or controlled atmosphere packaging. By replacing most of the oxygen inside the packaging with carbon dioxide and nitrogen, the growth of food spoilage organisms is slowed down so that food looks, tastes and smells fresh for much longer. Meat, for example, if left open to the air, soon turns brown as the red blood oxidises. Removing the oxygen keeps it looking red and fresh for longer. Vegetables, on the other hand, need to 'breathe' to keep them looking fresh, so specially designed gas-permeable films or microscropic holes let a controlled amount of oxygen into the sealed package. Vacuum-packaging keeps food fresh by removing all the oxygen and air.

To keep these foods safe it's vitally important for there to be strict hygiene during manufacturing, adequate refrigeration during transport and in the supermarket cabinet, and where appropriate, for foods to be thoroughly cooked. There's a risk of food poisoning if bacteria are not killed or if the food is contaminated during processing. Botulism is a potential problem, as the bacteria responsible grows in the absence of oxygen.

It can also be done on a larger scale – produce such as some apples, bananas and potatoes are stored in modified atmosphere chambers for weeks on end. It ensures an even supply of the fruit, but often at the expense of the taste and texture of really fresh produce.

Are we being misled about the freshness of such foods? Although modified atmosphere packaging has been around for many years, labelling has been long overdue. It's only recently that new EU rules mean companies must declare its use. Even so, it is coyly described with the words 'packed in a protective atmosphere'.

The Chemical Option

There's a whole host of chemicals which can be sprayed onto food to ensure that it looks fresher for longer. Potatoes, for example, are regularly doused with the toxic fungicide tecnazene, which stops potatoes sprouting. In theory there should be a safe interval between treatment and sale, but in the past excessive levels have been found in supermarket-bought potatoes. In some other countries you'll find notices that tell you if potatoes have been treated in this way, but not in the UK.

Similarly, fruit such as apples, pears, cherries, citrus fruits and bananas may be treated with chemical preservatives after harvest to delay spoilage. Some fungicides used have actually got E numbers (E230–233) but you won't find any labels at the fruit counter – fresh fruit and veg are exempt from having to make the declarations that apply to processed foods – even though some of these chemicals are suspected of causing cancer.

Freezing

How do you know that 'fresh' meat and poultry wasn't previously frozen? The answer is it's very difficult. In one Government survey, 44 samples out of 536 (8 per cent) were found to be previously frozen but not labelled as such.[6] The run-up to Christmas is a time when shops sometimes sell 'fresh' turkeys which have in fact been frozen. Not only is it a rip-off, as fresh turkeys command twice the price of frozen ones, but it could also be a safety hazard.

One loophole has been tightened up. Supermarkets can no longer advertise bread as 'freshly baked' if they use frozen ready-made dough, a court ruled, after Trading Standards Officers said it was misleading to customers. It should only be described as fresh if it was baked on the premises with fresh dough.

Cook-chilled Foods

The UK has led the way in the technological development of 'fresh' ready meals. It's called 'cook-chill' as the food is first cooked, which ensures food-poisoning bacteria are killed, and then speedily chilled. But it must be kept cold enough to prevent bacteria from growing again. Problems start if the temperature rises during storage, transport or while in supermarket chill cabinets. In the late 1980s there was much concern when the food poisoning bacteria listeria was found in some ready meals, and microwave ovens were found not to be heating foods thoroughly enough to kill the bacteria. New hygiene regulations are meant to ensure all such foods are kept at sufficiently low temperatures.

Food Irradiation

A few years ago food irradiation was being hailed as the latest way to keep food fresh for longer. But the idea of our food being bombarded with ionising radiation to make it last longer, funnily enough, didn't catch on with the British consumer. Despite the experts who were wheeled out to convince us it was all perfectly safe, hardly anyone was convinced that what we wanted or needed was food that might look fresh but was old, stale and contained fewer vitamins. Though the Government made food irradiation legal in 1991 only one UK company has a licence to do it – and that's only for herbs and spices.

But with tests to detect whether food has been irradiated still in development, it's hard to know whether other foods, irradiated abroad, are being imported and sold in the UK without proper labelling. By law all irradiated foods should be labelled, but spot checks have found unlabelled irradiated produce, mainly spices, on sale to the public. Leading supermarkets are investigating with their suppliers after the supermarkets were found to be selling unlabelled irradiated curry powder, chilli powder and paprika.

In 1992 Europe's big three irradiating countries, France, Belgium and the Netherlands, were jointly irradiating over 37,000 tonnes of food including seafood, frogs' legs, poultry and vegetables, and around 10,000 tonnes of herbs and spices. Yet with irradiated food not knowingly sold in European shops, the question remains as to where this food is ending up. There is speculation that much may end up as ingredients in processed or restaurant food.

Gas Ripening

Have you ever wondered why some supermarket fresh fruit looks good but, when you bite into it, is still unripe and flavourless? That's because much fruit, including bananas, pineapples, grapes and tomatoes, are picked unripe while they are still hard and easier to transport and then artificially ripened later in special chambers containing ethylene gas – the same gas that fruits give off naturally when they ripen. But the results are not often a great success – supermarkets say they sell unripe fruit so that we can let it ripen ourselves at home, but how many of us have found fruit going squidgy and mouldy before it ever ripens?

Tricks of the Trade

Ever since food was bought and sold, unscrupulous traders have tried to sell food that wasn't all it should be. Passing off food as a better quality product by swapping an important ingredient with a similar and cheaper alternative, or falsely describing it, is illegal. But even today consumers in shops, pubs and restaurants are being duped.

Food laws should protect us against illegal adulteration of food and we rely on the vigilant eyes of local food law enforcement officers to keep the scams in check. But as the tricks have become more sophisticated, ever more sophisticated analytical methods need to be developed to check exactly what is in our food. And it's not always easy to bring someone to book. The law says that it is an offence to use a description which is likely to mislead as to a food's nature, substance or quality. That sounds strong stuff, but enforcement officers complain that gaps in the law and vagueness about how it should be interpreted mean that it's not always easy to bring a case to court.

In 1992 the Government set up a programme of testing to check the authenticity of certain foods. They tested 874 samples of breaded scampi, battered and breaded fish, instant coffee and vegetable oils. And the results? Ninety-five – nearly 11 per cent – were illegally adulterated or falsely described.

Here are some of the tricks of the trade that have been uncovered.

Pasta – putting non-durum wheat in pasta which is described as 100 per cent durum wheat.

Fish – using fish mince in 'quality' fish products; using cheaper types of fish in breaded products like scampi.

Oil – mixing olive oil with poorer quality oil or other vegetable oils.

Cheese – using a cheese substitute instead of real cheese in pizzas and cheese sandwiches.

Instant coffee – adding other material than that from pure coffee beans, such as plant stems and husks.

Vanilla – mixing synthetic chemically-produced vanillin with, or swapping it for, vanilla.

Wine – adding too much sugar to increase alcohol content.

Whisky – refilling whisky bottles in pubs with a different and cheaper brand than the one shown on the label; diluting with water.

Rice – mixing other types of rice with rice sold as basmati rice.

Meat – adding offal to meat products but not declaring it on the label; selling frozen and thawed meat as 'fresh'; using mechanically recovered meat (MRM) in meat products sold as being made from meat pieces and not declaring it on the label; selling meat described as Halal containing pork; minced beef containing other meats such as pork and lamb; adding extra fat to joints of meat.

Bacon and ham – adding too much water and not declaring it on the label.

Mineral water – using artificial methods to carbonate water and describing the result as naturally carbonated.

Scampi – using other shellfish besides scampi, most commonly the less expensive warm water prawns, in scampi products sold in pubs and restaurants.

Yoghurt – using cow's milk in yoghurt described as sheep or goat's milk yoghurt.

Citrus fruit juices – adding ingredients not from citrus fruit.

Spices – selling irradiated spices as non-irradiated.

LEGAL ADULTERATION

All the above examples are illegal, but there's a whole range of tricks of the trade which are quite legal and which can deceive shoppers about what they are buying.

Selling Water Instead of Meat

When you buy meat, you could be buying up to 5 per cent added water – quite legally – with nothing on the label to tell you so. The Consumers' Association have found some hams with over 25 per cent water.[7]

Cuts of ham are put in a solution of salty water along with additives such as polyphosphates and gums which help to hold in extra water, often with the help of multi-needle injectors. Massaging and tumbling helps the ham to take up more water, and the release of protein helps to bind it all together when it's cooked. Ham must declare the amount of added water, but other products like sausages, which can contain up to a third added water, don't have to declare how much is added, just to list water in the ingredients. Added rusk is cheap and can absorb up to twice its weight in water, while phosphates help to hold the water in the sausage.

Most bacon contains some added water, but this need only be declared if it's more than 10 per cent – so bacon which claims to contain 'not more than 15 per cent added water' could quite legally contain up to 25 per cent added water.

Double-glazing

This is a favourite of frozen prawn sellers. Soak the prawns in water, freeze them and then spray more water on and freeze that too. Prawns don't need more than 20 per cent ice to keep them in good condition, but what they need and what they get can be two different things. Some producers quite legally add twice as much – double-glazing as it's known in the trade – and at present there's no obligation to tell shoppers. In one survey in 1993, half the samples of frozen prawns contained more than 25 per cent ice glaze; in the worst cases half of the weight was ice. And in one case, which was successfully prosecuted, ice made up a staggering 58 per cent.[8]

Getting More Water into Bread

Ever thought your bread was a bit soggy? Well, you were probably right. Bread is sold by weight and water is cheaper and heavier than flour. Virtually all mass-produced bread is made using the Chorleywood process. Instead of the traditional slower fermentation and kneading, this uses high-speed mechanical mixing and the addition of a higher proportion of water than traditionally made bread. There's no legal limit on the amount of water bread can contain.

An Optical Illusion

Batter and breadcrumbs can coat meat and fish, giving the impression that you are getting more for your money than you really are. If you are really lucky you can get batter and breadcrumbs together. Some chicken nuggets being sold for school dinners have been found to be only around one-third meat and two-thirds coating.[9]

Getting More Air into Ice Cream

Ice cream is sold by volume – so the more air you can get in there, the less real ingredients you need. Additives such as emulsifiers and stabilisers ensure there are over 240 million air cells in a single ounce of some ice creams. Margaret Thatcher was one of the scientists who helped to develop this process.

Fancy Packaging

Watch out for clever packaging that disguises just how much – or how little – you are buying. Luxury chocolates can be some of the worst offenders – their fancy packaging can come with a false base that makes the box look fuller than it is. And it's not just expensive items – plastic yoghurt and dessert pots can have a domed bottom to reduce the contents while allowing the pot to look larger. The solution? Don't be fooled by fancy packaging – always take a close look at the weight.

Downsizing

Here's a clever one – how many of us actually check the size of products we buy to the exact gram? And would we remember? The chances are we don't – and that's what canny manufacturers rely on. So here's how to do it – redesign the pack – charge the same amount (or even more) as before, but sell less by making the packet smaller. One juice manufacturer reduced the size of their pure orange juice carton from 1 litre to 750 ml and upped the price. They also made the smaller carton taller and thinner so that it actually looked larger!

Symbols for Selling

You'll often see foods and drinks adorned with logos, symbols and endorsements. But what do they mean, and are they a useful seal of approval or just another marketing ploy?

FAIRTRADE

Buying fairly traded foods ensures that more of the money you spend reaches the people who produce the food – typically small-scale farmers in developing countries. By ensuring that they receive a fair price for what they produce, communities can invest in health care, education and housing and are no longer subject to the mercies of the global market, which can wreck their livelihoods overnight.

You'll find the Fairtrade mark on some teas, coffee and chocolate. The most well-known is Cafédirect coffee. The Fairtrade Foundation, which administers the scheme, has been set up by OXFAM and other development agencies. Before awarding its stamp of approval the Foundation checks the working conditions and rechecks them, on average, once a year. Some products are now available in supermarkets while a wider range can be found in OXFAM shops or through many health food stores.

GREEN SYMBOLS

There's now an array of food trumpeting its 'green' and environmentally-friendly and animal-welfare credentials.

Vegetarian Symbols

The V logo on foods suitable for vegetarians can be helpful for people choosing a meat-free diet. Around 2,000 foods that carry the logo have been approved by the Vegetarian Society and do not contain meat, fish, animal fats, fish oil, intensively produced eggs or any ingredients tested on animals since 1986. The Society charges a licence fee. It does not normally test products but it does carry out random inspections. Many supermarkets have their own symbols, and their own standards, for identifying foods suitable for vegetarians. Some, for example, may permit intensively-produced eggs, while others will allow only free-range eggs.

Organic

There's a range of logos and symbols guaranteeing that a food is genuinely organic – that is, produced without chemical pesticides, fertilisers and, for animals, in less-intensive conditions without routine drugs or other additives added to feed. (*See 'Choosing Organic', page 158.*) The Soil Association is the most well-known of the certifying bodies in the UK, but all organic standards are laid down by law, with annual inspections.

Conservation Grade

This symbol is part of a scheme run by the Guild of Conservation Grade Food Producers and is a halfway house between conventional agriculture and totally organic. For cereals, fruit and vegetables there are controls on the chemicals which can be used, but these are not as strict as organic standards.

Freedom Food

Run by the RSPCA, you'll find this logo on some pork, chicken, bacon and eggs in some supermarkets. It's another halfway house scheme that aims to improve the conditions of intensively-reared animals but which falls short of organic standards, and the amount of freedom that animals have is less than you might think. Freedom Food eggs, for example, can be laid by chickens that have never experienced natural light.

Free-range

There are no legal definitions of free-range for meat such as pork, lamb or beef, and so labels claiming 'free-range' may be meaningless unless there are published definitions and, preferably, an independent certifying system. There are legal standards for free-range chickens and eggs, but these have been criticised for being too low – poultry can still be crowded into huge sheds with many birds never seeing the outdoors.

HEALTH AND FITNESS SYMBOLS

Sports Endorsements

Soft drinks may carry endorsements such as from the FA Premier League and the British Athletic Federation. Other products have been described as the 'official drink' of the World Cup or the Olympic Games. Apart from the apparent health endorsement by associating the products with top-class sports, some products actually go further – one drink claimed that 'the quality of the drink are those required by club nutritionists'. But take such claims with a pinch of salt – these kinds of endorsements are typically straightforward marketing deals.

Tooth-friendly

You'll find the tooth-friendly logo on some sweets, which means that they have been cleared as not causing tooth decay. The scheme is run in the UK by the British Dental Association and products are independently tested. It's a useful way of identifying sweets which won't harm teeth but, be warned, there may be a downside. The sweeteners that are used can have a laxative effect (*see page 52*) if you eat too much. And they can help to encourage a child's sweet tooth. Other retailers may have their own schemes such as own-brand confectionery labelled 'kind to teeth'.

Charity Endorsements

Another way to appeal to shoppers is to associate your product with a good cause. If it helps to create a warm feeling about a product then we're more likely to buy it rather than its rival. Charities may benefit by receiving a fee for the use of their name and an increased awareness of their cause, but in the end it's just a way to encourage us to buy one chocolate bar or packet of biscuits over another. Supermarkets have also got in on the act by helping schools, for example with computer equipment. It all helps to keep parents loyal to one particular chain.

2

Added Extras

Reading the ingredients list of some processed foods can seem like reading a chemistry book. There's often a whole host of ingredients that you wouldn't find in a recipe book, your kitchen cupboard or on supermarket shelves.

Everyone's Favourite?

INGREDIENTS

WHIPPING CREAM (WITH STABILISER: SODIUM ALGINATE), CHOCO-LATE FLAVOUR FLAKES (WITH EMULSIFIERS: SOYA LECITHIN, POLYG-LYCEROL POLYRINCINOLEATE), WHEATFLOUR, WATER, SUGAR, EGG, MANDARINS, MANDARIN JUICE, FAT REDUCED COCOA POWDER, RAISING AGENTS: DISODIUM DIHYDROGEN DIPHOSPHATE, SODIUM BICARBONATE; EMULSIFIERS: MONO- AND DIGLYCERIDES OF FATTY ACIDS; SKIMMED MILK POWDER, MODIFIED CORNSTARCH, ORANGE FLAVOUR CHOCOLATE FLAKES (WITH EMULSIFIERS: SOYA LECITHIN; COLOUR: BETA B-APOCAROTENAL), WHEY POWDER, STABILISER: GUAR GUM; CITRIC ACID, SALT.

The picture on the packet looks yummy, but not all the ingredients sound quite so appetising or familiar. They include a derivative of seaweed, an extract of castor oil, salts of phosphoric acid, and a gum made from pea seeds. If you haven't already guessed, this ingredients list belongs to a frozen gateau. Not just any ordinary gateau – this one declares on the box that it is 'hand finished'. To add a personal touch to industrial cake-making, the chocolate and orange flavour flakes (*NB 'flavour'* – no real chocolate or orange there, then) have been sprinkled on the top of the cake by hand. It's good to know someone cares!

Mystery Ingredients Explained

The mystery ingredients in our food can include additives and a whole range of other unfamiliar ingredients. Here are just some of them.

Annatto (E160b) – 'natural' yellow colouring made from tropical tree seeds, which can provoke allergic reactions.

Ascorbic acid (E300) – vitamin C. Used to prevent colours fading, to help bread to rise and to increase the shelf-life of beers.

Brown FK (E154) – the FK stands 'for kippers' as it's used to colour kippers and other smoked fish. One of the notorious 'azo dyes' which can trigger asthma and allergies in sensitive people.

Caffeine – occurs naturally in coffee, tea, cocoa and cola nuts. Also added to some soft drinks including colas and 'energy' drinks. Guarana also contains caffeine. Despite recommendations by Government advisors for an upper limit on caffeine in soft drinks, none has been implemented. Some soft drinks can contain 10 times more caffeine than others. High caffeine doses in children can lead to hyperactivity, disrupted sleep and withdrawal symptoms.

Calcium carbonate (E170) – chalk. Naturally occurring mineral used in white bread, biscuits, buns and cakes.

Calcium sulphate (E516) – plaster of Paris. Naturally occurring mineral which may be added to bread and used in beer making.

Caramel (E150) – most common food colouring – accounts for about 98 per cent of all colours used. Added to a huge range of foods from colas and chocolate to bread and beer. Also used as a flavouring. Not all caramel is 'burnt sugar', most is made chemically and it's relatively easy to exceed 'safe' limits for some types.

Carrageenan (E407) – seaweed extract used as a thickener and emulsifier in a wide range of foods.

Carboxylmethylcellulose (E466) – made from wood pulp and used as a bulking and gelling agent in many foods including cakes and desserts, ice cream, milk shakes, dips and spreads. Linked to flatulence and digestive discomfort.

Guar gum (E412) – extracted from pea seeds. Used as a thickener, emulsifier and fat-replacer in a wide range of foods.

Hydrogenated vegetable oil – artificially hardened vegetable fat, as artery-clogging as saturated fat.

Hydrolysed vegetable protein – a close relative of monosodium glutamate which gives a meaty taste to many processed foods such as stock cubes and soups, vegetarian and meat products. Some types have been found to develop a toxic contaminant, chloropropanol, during processing. Now manufacturers must ensure that foods and ingredients no longer contain the harmful contaminant.

Maltodextrin – low-cost, low-nutrient refined starch which absorbs water easily to make an instant gluey paste. Also used to stick envelopes and postage stamps.

Monosodium glutamate (E621) – flavour-enhancer first isolated from seaweed in Japan in 1908 and called 'umami', meaning deliciousness. Now mainly made by fermentation of molasses. Has caused controversy as there are some suggestions it can cause 'Chinese Restaurant Syndrome' – headaches, palpitations and dizziness after eating meals. Banned in foods for babies and young children, but generally thought to be safe for adults.

Shellac (E904) – an insect secretion used to wax fruit and glaze sweets and cake decorations.

Tartrazine (E102) – once widely-used yellow 'azo' dye which became the focus of concerns about additives, particularly in foods for children. Reports of adverse reactions more common than for any other synthetic colour.

ADDITIVES

Each year on average we eat nearly 3 kg of food additives – and that's an average. Depending on your diet you could be eating an awful lot more.

All in all there are about 400 food additives – plus over 3,500 substances allowed to be used as flavours which have not been given an E number. A great many additives are substances that you'd never use in home cooking. Many are an aid to food manufacturers – from emulsifiers and stabilisers, which help fats and oils to mix with water and make a creamier texture, to anti-caking agents, bulking agents, anti-foaming agents, glazing agents and flour improvers. Only a small number of additives are used to help preserve food. These are mainly the preservatives – which slow down the growth of harmful micro-organisms and antioxidants to prevent fat and oils from going rancid. Some of the antioxidants are actually used to prevent colour and flavour additives from fading.

E Numbers

Nearly all additives which have to be declared on labels (with the exception of flavours) now have E numbers as shown below. The letter 'E' shows that additives have been approved for use throughout the European Union.

Until recently, different countries had different rules over which additives were and were not allowed. In the UK we permitted many more additives than some other countries. For example, we allowed

---

16 artificial colours to be used, while France, Belgium and the US permitted only permitted 11, and Norway none at all. But now there's a common agreement for the whole of the European Union.

It was hailed as a triumph for Britain when we were allowed to keep artificial red colours in sausages and artificial sweeteners in crisps. Consumer groups wanted to see the list of additives shortened, but the food industry fought tooth and nail to keep them all – with the result that we now have more additives allowed and even some old banned additives re-permitted (*see 'Cyclamates' Are Back, page 51*). However, limits were set for some additives on the maximum amounts allowed in foods, and some foods were banned from containing certain additives.

Colours: E100–180

Preservatives: E200–297

Antioxidants: E300–321

Emulsifiers, stabilisers and thickeners: E322–495

Processing aids: E500–585

Flavour enhancers: E620–640

Glazing agents: E900–914

Flour treatments, improvers and bleaching agents:
E920–928

Packing gases: E941–948

Sweeteners: E950–967

Miscellaneous additives: E999–1518

Flavours – no E numbers

Going Underground

It's increasingly difficult to find E numbers in ingredients lists. The frozen gateau above contains a number of additives, but instead of giving the E numbers the manufacturer has chosen to list the chemical names of the additives.

As more shoppers look out for E numbers on ingredients lists and avoid foods with a long list of them, a growing number of manufacturers use only the chemical name of the additives rather than the E number in the hope that we won't take as much notice. Consumer groups say manufacturers should be obliged to declare the E number as well as the name.

Do All Additives Have to Be Listed on Food Labels?

The general rule is yes, but like all rules there are exceptions. Flavourings don't have to be listed by name, and certain additives used as processing aids escape a listing altogether. These include:

- solvents, used to dilute other additives such as colourings and to extract flavours;
- enzymes used in food processing;
- processing aids, such as those used to stop ingredients sticking to machinery and baking trays (and which may remain in the food);
- packaging gases used to prolong the life of fresh foods.

Then there's the foods which are exempt from having to declare *any* of their ingredients, including additives. These include:

- wine and alcoholic drinks
- some confectionery and chocolate
- cheese, butter, most milk and cream products
- unwrapped foods such as bread or cakes
- take-away foods
- eggs and farmed fish (may contain dyes fed to chickens and fish to enhance colour)
- citrus fruits and apples treated with preservatives on skins.

Do We Need Additives?

We are often told that additives are necessary to keep food safe. Yet less than 1 per cent of additives used are preservatives which stop the growth of food-poisoning bacteria. These are important in keeping processed foods safe, but it's misleading to argue that preservatives justify all food additive use.

In fact the vast majority of additives are used for cosmetic reasons – to make food look more colourful, sometimes to disguise the lack of real ingredients, to give it a stronger or a sweeter taste or a creamier texture.

It's true that without so many additives we could not have the wide variety of processed foods we now have. Without emulsifiers, margarines and spreads would separate into oil and water, while flour improvers make the texture of bread and cakes lighter. But from a nutritional point of view it can be argued that less processed foods wouldn't be such a bad thing. It's processed foods that provide us with hefty doses of fat, salt and sugar – often disguised by additives so it's hard to tell exactly what we're eating, let along whether it's good for us.

Additives are only approved if there is considered to be a 'need' for them. But whether we 'need' so many additives is really down to food companies. They can argue they 'need' an additive to make their food more colourful, attractive or tasty or so they can make a food more cheaply.

Are Additives Safe?

Many people are concerned about the safety of food additives, particularly where babies and children are concerned. But with several hundred approved additives it is difficult to generalise. Certainly one additive that there are no safety doubts over is E300 – ascorbic acid – which is chemically identical to vitamin C. All additives have to be approved as safe before they can be used in foods and there are often limits on the amounts that can be used in individual foods. But despite these checks health concerns remain over some additives (*see 'Possible Problem Additives', page 44*).

Some additives may cause specific problems such as asthma, rashes, hyperactivity or other intolerant or allergic reactions in people who are sensitive. Just as some people may be sensitive to wheat, nuts or dairy products, some people, including children, may be sensitive to some additives such as the now notorious artificial 'azo dyes' such as the orange colour tartrazine. (*See 'Allergy and Intolerance', page 116.*) Other additives have been linked to cancers, reproductive problems or other damage in laboratory test animals. Yet the effects on humans of amounts generally consumed in the diet over a long period are not necessarily known. Margins of safety are built into permitted levels of use, but it is difficult to apply results on rats to humans. In addition, the possible synergistic, cocktail effect of a mixture of additives in the body cannot be fully assessed.

For the majority of consumers direct health risks from food additives may be low when compared with other health risks from food, such as the risk of heart disease from an unhealthy diet or the risk of allergy from common foods such as peanuts, wheat, dairy foods and shellfish. But that is no reason to expose people to additional risks. Given that absolute safety can rarely be guaranteed, it is vital that safety assessments are thorough and give the benefit of any doubt to consumers rather than to the food industry.

Master of Disguises

Additives pose probably their greatest risk to our health in the way they are used to help to disguise cheap ingredients as good food and persuade us to eat foods that are high in fats, processed starches, salt and sugar. Additives and the wonders of modern food technology turn these basic ingredients into a multitude of 'different' foods – from cakes, biscuits, snacks and sweets to noodles, sauces and soups. But what we get, more often than not, are processed foods, stuck together with additives, that are low nutritional value.

Here are some examples of the way in which additives can disguise what we are eating:

- Colours can disguise the lack of real ingredients. Yellow colouring can give the impression of eggs in custard powder. Colours in fruit drinks and yoghurts can disguise the lack of real fruit. Red colours in cheap meat products can disguise fat as lean meat.
- Flavourings turn foods with poor nutrition (for example extruded products such as savoury snacks), into exciting lunchbox must-haves

for children. Lemonade need contain no real lemon, beef and tomato pot noodle no real beef or tomato.

- Flavour enhancers typically enhance the flavour, not of real ingredients, but of artificial flavours.
- Additives such as emulsifiers, stabilisers and thickeners help bulk out food with really cheap ingredients – water and air.
- Mechanically recovered meat, used in sausages and other cheap meat products, is a grey, porridge-like slurry – not what most of us would call meat. But the addition of additives – preservatives to keep the bacteria in check, emulsifiers and thickeners to make it firm and chunky, and colourings to make it pink and lean-looking, make for an end-product unrecognisable from what most of us would call meat.
- Offcuts, flakes and scraps of fish can be blended, minced and reformed with the help of water-absorbing polyphosphate additives to be turned into fish fingers and other coated fish products. Legally they can be called **fish steaks** and **fish portions**, but not **whole fillets** – so check the label carefully.
- Various additives and 'improvers' not used in traditional bread-making help pump much mass-produced bread full of air and water. Colours such as caramel are used to make bread look brown and healthier.

Possible Problem Additives

ADDITIVE	NAME	POSSIBLE PROBLEMS
Colours:		
E102, E104, E107, E110, E122, E123, E124, E127, E128, E129, E131, E132, E133, E142, E151, E154, E155	Azo dyes made from coal tar – used as textile dyes. Includes tartrazine E102	Asthma, rashes, hyperactivity. Some have been linked to cancer in test animals.
E120	Cochineal (insect extract)	Food intolerance.
E150	Caramel	Some forms may damage genes, reduce white blood cells and destroy vitamin B_6.
E160(b)	Annatto (tree seed extract)	May cause asthma, rashes.
E161(g)	Canthaxanthin	Eye damage – banned in food but can be used in feed to colour egg yolks and farmed fish without labelling.
Preservatives:		
E210–E219	Benzoate preservatives	May cause asthma, rashes, hyperactivity.
E220–E228	Sulphite preservatives	May provoke asthma, destroys vitamin B_1.
E230–E233	Preservatives used on citrus fruit/apple skins (not declared on labels)	Can provoke adverse reactions in sensitive people.

| E249–E262 | Nitrites/nitrite preservatives | Linked to cancers. |

Antioxidants:

| E310–E312 | Gallates | May cause intolerant reactions. |
| E320, E321 | BHA, BHT | May cause rashes and hyperactivity. Linked to cancer in test animals. |

Emulsifiers, thickeners, etc.:

| E407 | Carrageenan (Irish Moss) | Linked to ulcers in colon and foetal damage in test animals. |
| E413 | Tragacanth gum | Allergic reactions. |

Sweeteners:

| E420, E421, E953, E965, E966, E967 | Bulk sweeteners e.g. sorbitol, mannitol, isomalt | Laxative effect. |
| E950, E951, E952, E954 | Intense sweeteners acesulfame-K, aspartame, cyclamates, saccharin | Questions remain over safety. Some linked to cancer and neural problems. |

Shh, It's a Secret

Flavourings make up about 20 per cent of all the additives we consume by weight – that's about 2 g of flavours a day, or 100 times the amount of vitamin C most people consume. Yet when it comes to flavours, what we are eating is a secret. There isn't an approved list of flavouring additives and they don't have to be tested for safety in the same way that other additives do. If you're unlucky enough to be sensitive to a particular chemical, there's no way you can tell which foods it's in.

Babies and Young Children

There are special rules for additives used in foods for babies and young children. Such foods aren't allowed to contain a number of additives, including all of the possible problem additives listed above. This sounds reassuring but the official line is they are banned – not because they are unsafe for youngsters – but because they are not 'needed'. However there are plenty of foods eaten by children from a very young age – and often made to appeal to them, such as fizzy drinks, savoury snacks, crisps, desserts, sausages, fish fingers, sweets, ice cream and lollies – which are jammed packed with these banned additives.

This is possible because there's a loophole in the law which means that the rule only applies to foods and drinks that are *specially prepared* for babies and young children – and that means baby foods, drinks and formula milks. Because other foods for children are consumed by older children (and some adults) they are not subject to this law.

A Long Wait

In much official decision-making about food safety the interests of food manufacturers have come before those of consumers.

Canthaxanthin

It took the UK Government over seven years to ban the colouring additive canthaxanthin (E161g) from food after the Food Advisory Committee said it should be banned immediately. Research had found that the chemical could damage the retina of the eye. It's still permitted in feed for farmed fish, such as salmon, as well as in chicken feed where it's used to colour egg yolks – but you'll find nothing on the label to tell you so.

Erythrosine
It also took seven years for the virtual ban on the red dye erythrosine (E127) to be implemented. As a suspected carcinogen and mutagen it can now only be used in cocktail and candied cherries. Yet even though the writing was on the wall for the chemical, some well-known manufacturers continued to use it right up until the last moment it was legal, often in sweets for young children.

Mineral Hydrocarbon Oils and Waxes
In another case it took the Government over four years to implement its ban on toxic mineral hydrocarbon oils and waxes, by-products of the petrochemical industry, used to grease tins for bread-making, to wax citrus fruits and to prevent dried fruits from sticking together.

In 1989 the Ministry of Agriculture, Fisheries and Food (MAFF) announced in a press release its intention to ban mineral hydrocarbons in food 'as soon as possible'. Yet it was 1993 before action was taken. MAFF had gone along with the oil industry's delaying tactics and let them do more safety research. When this was finally available it confirmed what had already been suspected: the oils were definitely toxic. Some of the waxes are still allowed in chewing gum, and the wax rind on some cheeses, but official advice is don't swallow it and don't eat it with other foods, particularly chocolate. But you won't find this warning on chewing gum packs.

Boozy Secrets

Want to know what's in your favourite tipple? Well, you can't. For no good reason, except the reluctance of manufacturers, we're denied the right to know, which for some people could pose a risk to their life.

The majority of manufacturers use additives to improve the head on beers, increase shelf-life and to impart better colour and flavours. That can add a cocktail of artificial sweeteners, enzymes, stabilisers and sulphite preservatives. Sulphites are the only additives known to have caused deaths. They can bring on headaches and cause life-threatening asthma attacks in some people. The worst offenders are cheap wines often highly laced with sulphites. In the US they must be labelled, but not in the UK.

There's a popular belief that low-alcohol drinks are 'full of additives'. Take a look at the ingredients list and you can often see why. But at least you can see what's in them – low-alcohol drinks, like most other foods and drinks, must declare their ingredients.

Naturally So

In the 1980s when consumers began to wise up to additives in food, many manufacturers began to change from using artificial colours to so-called natural ones. But what can pass as natural isn't always so reassuring.

When the yellow artificial dye, tartrazine, got such a bad name for causing hyperactivity and allergic reactions, many food manufacturers started to use the natural food colour, annatto – E160(b). What few people realise is that this 'natural' additive can trigger allergic reactions itself.

'No artificial flavours' may give the impression that flavours come from real ingredients. But they may not. So-called 'nature-identical' flavours are laboratory-made chemicals which imitate those found in nature. A 'nature-identical' strawberry flavour, for example, will never have been near a strawberry in its life.

And while many colourings may come from 'natural' sources, their use may not be so natural. Red colouring from beetroot (betanin E162), for example, is natural, but not necessarily what you'd expect in a strawberry yoghurt.

FREE-FROM ARTIFICIAL THIS AND THAT

Some retailers and food manufacturers have reduced the number of artificial additives they use in foods. And of course they want shoppers to know, so they proclaim it in big letters on the front of the packet '*Free from artificial flavourings, colours and preservatives'*. It sounds reassuring, but is it really as good as it sounds? Not always. Take a close look at the small print in the ingredients list – it could still contain 'natural' flavours and colours – some of which are just as suspect as artificial ones, as well as additives that aren't flavours, colours or preservatives – artificial sweeteners, for example. So don't always believe that the big print tells the whole story.

Nitrites

Nitrites are used, mainly in meat products, as a preservative to prevent the growth of food-poisoning bacteria. Nitrites have been linked with stomach cancer. Back in 1978 Government advisors recommended that their use should be eliminated from food 'as soon as practicable'. That didn't happen, but the EU recently set a maximum level of 100 mg/kg nitrite in cooked meats. Some manufacturers will have to reduce the amount they add to comply. One survey by the Consumers' Association[1] found British hams to have high levels of nitrites compared with products from other European countries – some near to or exceeding the EU limit. One of the reasons nitrites remain popular with manufacturers is that they have an additional cosmetic effect of adding a pink colour to meat products, especially raw products and hams where colourings are not permitted. They are banned in foods for babies.

Sweetness and Lite

Take a close look at the label and you'll find artificial sweeteners in all kinds of foods, even savoury ones. It's not just 'diet' or 'low-calorie' drinks where you'll find them, they crop up in everything from regular squashes, fizzy drinks, jellies, ice lollies and desserts to baked beans, snacks, soup, sauces, pasta and pickles. You'll even find them in most popular brands of toothpaste.

While other countries have historically limited the foods in which artificial sweeteners can be used, the British food industry has taken to them like a duck to water. So much so that, according to 1992 figures, we Brits consumed more aspartame than all the rest of Europe together; our saccharin consumption accounted for a third of the European total.

There are two types of artificial sweeteners – the intense ones such as saccharin, aspartame, acesulfame-K and cyclamate – and the so-called bulk sweeteners which include sorbitol, isomalt and mannitol. These are typically used in 'tooth-friendly' confectionery and in some so-called diabetic foods.

Are Artificial Sweeteners Safe?

Despite their approval as safe, some questions remain about the safety of several artificial sweeteners.

- **Acesulfame-K (trade name Sunett)** is facing demands in the US for safety reassessment over fears that it might cause cancer.[2]
- **Aspartame (trade name NutraSweet)** produces phenylalanine (a problem for sufferers of phenylketonuria), though products now carry warning labels. Aspartame has been linked anecdotally to neurological problems and migraines,[3] though this has not been proven and is disputed by the manufacturers. There have also been criticisms by independent scientists of the safety testing for aspartame.[4] Recent US research identifies aspartame as 'a promising candidate to explain the recent increase in incidence and degree of malignancy of brain tumours'.[5]
- **Saccharin** is linked to bladder cancer in test animals. In the US products containing saccharin must carry the warning: 'Use of this product may be hazardous to your health. This product contains saccharin which has been determined to cause cancer in laboratory animals.' Some people, especially young children, may exceed 'safe' levels of consumption (*see page 115*). And it's not just children who are at risk of consuming too much saccharin. People with diabetes and others who use table-top sweeteners are also at risk of exceeding safe limits.
- **Cyclamates** were banned in 1968 because of cancer fears. Now they are back despite research which shows they can shrivel the testicles of laboratory animals. They are now permitted at levels which

independent scientists say could put men and boys at risk. It's frighteningly easy for young children to exceed 'safe' levels – just a third of a litre of soft drink (the size of a regular can) containing cyclamates could put a four-year-old over the limit.

Cyclamates Are Back

In 1996 MAFF rewrote the rules when pressure from manufacturers and for harmonisation with European additive laws led MAFF to re-permit the artificial sweetener sodium cyclamate to be used in soft drinks, desserts, confectionery, chewing gum and food supplements – even though tests on laboratory animals showed it could damage testicles.

With a range of artificial sweeteners now available to manufacturers it's hard to see why we need to have another one, particularly one which carries such a risk. MAFF's scientific advisers on the Committee on Toxicity of Chemicals in Food, Consumer Products and the Environment (COT) were concerned when new research found 'irreversible testicular atrophy' in rats fed the chemical. Subsequent tests on monkeys also showed damage to the testes and lowered levels of the male hormone, testosterone. But, by claiming that the monkey reaction was 'less severe' than that in rats and that the reactions 'were more likely to be reversible', the sweetener was effectively cleared for use.

Then, not only did COT ignore the monkey data when setting new safety levels for the chemical, they also only allowed for a safety factor of 10 to account for the differences between rats and humans – 10 times less than the safety factor of 100 that is conventionally used.

Now we're told it's safe for everyone to consume up to 6 mg of cyclamate per kg of body weight every day. Yet it is frighteningly easy to exceed this maximum, especially for young children. A four-year-old weighing 17 kg is in theory safe to consume 102 mg of cyclamate a day. Yet with soft drinks permitted to contain 400 mg of cyclamate per litre, *just a third of a litre* can contain more than the maximum amount a 17kg child should consume. Children are most at risk of exceeding the safety limits because of their lower body weights, but it's also relatively easy for an adult to consume too much. By drinking just three cans of soft drink sweetened with cyclamate you could unwittingly exceed the acceptable daily limit. MAFF says you'd have to do it every day of your life to be at risk – but, quite apart from the fact that there are some people who may drink this much, why should we be exposed to such risks?

The advantage of cyclamate for food manufacturers is that it is cheap. But should MAFF be playing Russian roulette with the future health of our children for the sake of allowing food companies to make a few pence extra on a bottle of squash? All foods and soft drinks containing artificial sweeteners now have to declare the fact on the label. But you'll still have to read the small print to see exactly which sweetener, or cocktail of chemical sweeteners, it contains.

Sweeteners on the Label

It should now be much easier to identify foods and drinks which contain artificial sweeteners. From July 1997 the law says that all products containing artificial sweeteners must declare the fact next to the name of the product. But some soft drinks companies are circumventing the spirit of the law. Instead of putting the declaration 'with sweetener' next to the name on the front of bottles, they are repeating the name on the back or side of the pack and hiding away the sweeteners declaration in small print.

If the sweeteners include aspartame (NutraSweet) then the label must include a warning for people who suffer from the disorder phenylketonuria; if the sweeteners include any of the bulk sweeteners such as sorbitol or isomalt, then the label must warn of the possible laxative effects.

Shh, It's a Secret

No safety data on additives is made public – until after the approval procedure is complete. That means that independent scientists, consumer organisations and the general public have no access to the information on which decisions are made when it matters – at the time the decision is being taken, when they could influence the outcome. In the US things are different. All safety data is publicly available at all times. In this way the US Center for Science in the Public Interest could get access to flawed safety data on the controversial fat-free-fat, Olestra – *see page 129*. They passed it on to British consumer organisations who have in this case been able to question its safety and advisability during the UK approval process.

CONTAMINANTS IN FOOD

There are additives which are added intentionally to food, and there are others which get added unintentionally – as contaminants. The scares about phthalates in baby milk (*see page 107*) and dioxins in breastmilk are just two examples of unwanted chemicals getting into food.

Others have been known to come from packaging around food – clingfilm in particular has caused some worries. That's because some of the chemicals in clingfilm can migrate into foods, particularly fatty foods. The main worry is chemical plasticisers used to keep the film flexible. Since clingfilm became almost indispensable in many households, the Government's Committee on Toxicity became worried about the dramatic increase in our unwitting consumption of these largely untested chemicals. While all food additives must be thoroughly tested for safety, the same is *not* true of chemicals used in packaging.

The advice on the safe use of plastic film is:

- don't wrap fatty foods in plastic films
- don't use film in direct contact with food in a microwave oven
- never use film in a conventional oven

Gender-bender Chemicals

It's now becoming known that many chemicals used in modern life can mimic the female hormone oestrogen. These chemicals, known as endocrine disrupters, include some pesticides and chemicals used in detergents and plastics. They have been dubbed 'gender-bender' chemicals by the media because of the theory that these chemicals are responsible for the sex-change effects on wildlife and also the declining sperm count in men. But the ill-health effects may go further. Evidence is increasing that suggests a link between increased human exposure to these chemicals and reproductive and sexual development disorders, reduced fertility and even some cancers in men and women. Sperm counts in men have fallen by 50 per cent since 1940, while during the same period testicular cancer has doubled in most industrialised countries.

Even more worrying is that it's the developing foetus which may be at most risk. The balance between male and female hormones is critical at this stage of human development; any hormonal disruption in the foetus and early childhood seems to be more potent than in adulthood.

And how are these chemicals getting into our body? Well, it's mainly as contamination of the food we eat and the water we drink. In 1995 the Medical Research Council called for urgent research to assess the risks and identify the causes. However, such research could take years and independent scientists have criticised the Government for complacency in failing to act to restrict the use of oestrogenic chemicals now.

Oestrogen-mimics at Work

At least 37 chemicals have been identified as being able either to mimic oestrogens in the human body or to interfere with the various systems that regulate sex hormones. Many are chemical pollutants which enter the food chain and our drinking water and accumulate in fat tissues in humans and animals. These chemicals include:

Phthalates – so commonly used in plastics that they have become one of the most abundant man-made environmental pollutants. In 1996 phthalates were found in baby milks. MAFF caused a furore when it refused to name the brands that were affected. While saying that the levels were perfectly safe, the Government has asked manufacturers to find out where the phthalates are coming from and to reduce the levels. Other tests have found that phthalates from the printing ink used on packaging have contaminated foods such as cakes and biscuits, sausages, vegetable fat and gravy granules, some at levels that exceed safety limits.

Bisphenol-A – another oestrogen-mimicking chemical used to coat the inside of food tins, bottle tops and water pipes. The chemical has been found to leach from tins into vegetables such as asparagus, sweetcorn and peas.

Pesticides – some pesticides such as organochlorine pesticides commonly used as insecticides and fungicides, as well as the notorious pesticide DDT, which is banned in many western countries, but still occasionally turns up in food.

PCBs and dioxins – most dioxins come from the burning of wastes containing organochlorine compounds, like PVC plastics and treated wood, which can then contaminate farm land and food such as milk and meat. The US Environmental Protection Agency says that levels of dioxins in our bodies are already high enough to cause ill-health. Dioxins have been found in breastmilk though levels have fallen over the last decade. Also, higher-than-recommended levels have been found in some fish oil dietary supplements.

Phytoestrogens – these naturally-occurring oestrogen-mimics are found in high levels in plants such as soya. There is some evidence that phytoestrogens may be beneficial in protection against cancer in adults, but may possibly be harmful when fed to young babies (*see 'Soya Baby Milks, page 107*).

The pill – the contraceptive pill contains synthetic oestrogen and there have been fears that it may contaminate water supplies. While it has been detected in water sources it is not thought to be in significant concentrations – environmental pollutants seem to be far greater sources of oestrogenic chemicals.

Natural Contaminants

Aflatoxin

Some nuts such as peanuts, brazil and pistachio nuts and dried figs are susceptible to contamination with a toxic mould known as aflatoxin. Aflatoxins can cause cancer and limits have been set on the amounts that foods can contain, although occasionally foods – including peanut butter – have been found with higher levels. Make sure you use such foods well within 'best before' dates.

Patulin

In 1993 unacceptably high levels of patulin – a residue from mould on apples which is mutagenic – were found in some brands of apple juice. While MAFF discussed the results with the manufacturers, they kept consumer organisations and the general public in the dark. MAFF only published the results after they were leaked to the press, and then refused to name the affected brands. Companies cannot be prosecuted for exceeding maximum levels, as these levels are not bound by law. Follow-up monitoring has found the majority of juices to be within safe levels, though a small number continue to exceed it, mainly the cloudy types of apple juice not made from concentrates.

3

Shopping for Health

Most of us say we want to eat more healthily. The good news is that we are becoming much more interested in our health and the food we eat. A survey by the Consumers' Association found that the majority of shoppers – 61 per cent – say that they consider nutrition and health when shopping for food.[1] Yet the bad news is that as a nation we still eat too much fat, salt and added sugar, our intakes of fruit and vegetables are just a fraction of our Southern European neighbours', and we're getting fatter. So what's going on?

Many people think they are eating more healthily than they actually are, while others are confused. And it's not difficult to see why. As this chapter will show, it's all too easy for food manufacturers to pull the wool over our eyes with healthy-sounding claims and advertising that doesn't always stand up to scrutiny. This chapter will sort the health from the hype.

You Are What You Eat

Diet-related disease and illness are major causes of premature death in the UK. Despite some improvements, the UK, and particularly Scotland, are still near the top of countries with the most deaths from heart disease. Heart and circulatory disease is Britain's biggest killer, accounting for nearly 300,000 deaths a year; diet can also be a factor in some cancers and many other health problems.

Fats

Top of most people's hit list is fat. Fat's got a bad name. It's high in calories, it's bad for your heart and we eat too much of it. Official health advice is that fat should make up no more than 33 per cent of our daily energy intake. As a nation we *average* 39 per cent.

What may be surprising is that not all fat is bad – there are good fats as well. So how do you sort the healthy from the artery clogging?

GOOD FATS, BAD FATS

With words like 'saturated', 'polyunsaturated', 'monounsaturates' and 'cholesterol' being bandied about, and claims made for the health benefits of one over another, it's easy to be confused. One of the main reasons why we should be concerned about the amount and type of fat in our diet is its effect on our cholesterol level. Too much of the wrong type of fat can increase the cholesterol in our blood and therefore increase the risk of heart disease.

But before checking out the different types of fat, it's important to understand a little more about cholesterol and to distinguish between cholesterol in blood and cholesterol in food.

Cholesterol in Blood

The important risk measurement for heart disease is raised cholesterol levels in the blood. However, it may come as a surprise to learn that not all cholesterol in the blood is bad. That's because there are two types. LDL (low-density lipoprotein) cholesterol is the bad stuff because it tends to fur up your arteries with fatty deposits, increasing your risk of blood clots and blockage of the arteries. But there's also good cholesterol – HDL (high-density lipoprotein) cholesterol. This kind helps to carry cholesterol *away* from arteries to the liver where it is safely broken down. We need some cholesterol – too little can actually be harmful – but what is important is getting the balance right between LDL and HDL. Cutting down on fats in the diet, particularly the 'bad' fats such as saturated fat and trans fatty acids, and replacing some with 'better' fats, along with taking regular exercise, can help to increase levels of good HDL cholesterol relative to 'bad' LDL.

Cholesterol in Food

Some foods such as eggs, offal and shellfish naturally contain cholesterol, but the effect of this cholesterol in raising blood cholesterol levels is much less than the influence of 'bad' fats such as saturated fats or trans fatty acids. Latest advice says it's fine to eat these cholesterol-containing foods in moderation – for eggs that's no more than one a day.

For this reason you should treat 'low cholesterol' claims on food with caution. Such claims are misleading because they confuse dietary cholesterol with levels of cholesterol in the blood. Some foods correctly claiming to be 'low cholesterol' could actually contain high levels of saturated fat – a much bigger risk factor in increasing cholesterol in the blood. Cutting down on saturated fat is the key to cutting blood cholesterol, rather than worrying too much about foods which contain it.

Bad Fats

Saturated Fatty Acids

Saturated fats increase the risk of heart disease by encouraging the body to produce more bad, LDL, cholesterol. Some cancers such as breast and colon cancer are also linked to high intakes of saturated fats. Saturates are found mainly in foods of animal origin such as meat and dairy products; 'tropical' oils such as palm oil and coconut oils are also highly saturated, though there is some evidence that these may be less harmful than animal fats. Also watch out for processed foods such as biscuits and pastries, which may contain lard, animal fats or tropical oils. Current advice is to reduce consumption of saturates.

Trans Fatty Acids

Trans fats are made by artificially hardening healthier vegetable or fish oils through a process called hydrogenation. Trans fats are just as bad as saturated fats. They can increase bad, LDL, cholesterol and lower good, HDL, cholesterol. Watch out for hydrogenated or partially hydrogenated fats/oils, often found in margarines, biscuits, cakes and many other processed foods. Unlike saturates, the amount of trans fats isn't declared on detailed nutritional labels. This means that some foods, such as margarines, can have a healthier reputation than they deserve.

Tracking Down Trans Fats

For years margarine manufacturers claimed the high ground in the health battle against butter. But their healthy 'vegetable oil' image took a knock when it was discovered that margarine manufacturers were using a type of fat which was just as bad for health as saturated dairy fats in butter. The culprits are trans fatty acids (or trans fats for short) which are formed when liquid vegetable oils are artificially hardened, or hydrogenated, making them more useful for food processors. Trans fats are rarely found in nature, and what is now known is that they, too, can raise blood cholesterol levels and increase the risk of heart disease.

And it's not only many margarines and spreads which contain hydrogenated vegetable oils. They have crept into a surprisingly wide range of processed and fried foods – from biscuits, cakes, pastries and breakfast cereals to baby foods, sliced bread, fast food and even vegetarian sausages.

Avoiding trans fats can be difficult and calls for looking closely at the label. Watch out for hydrogenated or partially hydrogenated oils, hardened or vegetable fat, vegetable suet or margarine listed as an ingredient. With take-away foods it's even harder to tell as there are no ingredient labels. Some companies use hydrogenated oils, particularly for frying chips, while others don't.

By a quirk of law it's actually illegal to declare how many trans fatty acids are in products unless a 'low in trans fats' claim is made. Many nutritionists believe that trans fats should be declared on labels along with saturated fat. By adding the two together, lard, butter and solid vegetable oils score lowest for health, while soft, lower-fat spreads score better. The best advice is to use all fats, oils and spreads sparingly.

Polyunsaturated Fatty Acids

Despite all the hype about polyunsaturated fats, particularly from the margarine and spread manufacturers, not all types actually fall into the 'good' fats category, although they are certainly healthier than 'bad' fats such as saturates.

There are two types of polyunsaturates – omega-6s and omega-3s – which act differently in the body.

Medium Fats

Omega-6 Polyunsaturates

Omega-6s include linoleic acid, found in vegetable oils such as sunflower oil and margarines and spreads made with it. Small amounts are essential for health, and substituting saturates with polyunsaturates does lower 'bad' LDL cholesterol levels – but too much can reduce the amount of 'good' HDL cholesterol. High levels may also be associated with other health problems. The current advice is not to increase your consumption of omega-6 polyunsaturates.

Good Fats

Monounsaturated Fats

Monounsaturates are found mainly in olive oil, rapeseed oil, avocados and nuts. One of the theories of why the Mediterranean diet is so healthy is the high level of olive oil used (along with the greater consumption of fresh vegetables and fruit). It is still not clear exactly how monounsaturates are beneficial, but they are thought to keep up levels of 'good' HDL cholesterol. Yet despite encouragement from 'Mediterranean Diet' cookery books, we should be cautious about pouring the olive oil too liberally. We are still advised to cut oils and fats overall, and monounsaturates have as many calories as any other fat.

Omega-3 Polyunsaturates

There are two types of omega-3s – short chain omega-3s, which include α-linolenic acid (found in linseed, rapeseed and soyabean oil), and long-chain omega-3s (such as DHA and EPA, found in fish oils). We're advised to double our intake of long-chain omega-3s. Not only can they protect against heart disease but they can be of value in helping to treat inflammatory diseases such as rheumatoid arthritis. Good sources include oily fish such as mackerel, herring, pilchard, sardine, tuna, trout and salmon. Eating oily fish twice a week is recommended. Some foods now come fortified with fish oils, though beware of some claims (*see page 84*). Fish oil supplements are available.

In babies n-6 fatty acids such as DHA are thought to be essential for optimal brain, neural and visual development. They are found in breastmilk. Most formula milks do not provide the full range.

LOW FAT, HIGH PRICES

Alongside the regular artery-clogging foods, the chances are that there's now a 'reduced fat', 'low-fat' or 'lite' alternative. It's all a question of choice, we're told – we can now choose whether to pig out or feel pious. But with companies typically charging a premium price for the 'healthier' versions, it's a limited choice.

A survey of lower-fat foods by the Food Commission found that prices of many were significantly higher than regular products.[2] Reduced-fat sausages, burgers, ready meals, crisps, biscuits, ice cream and yoghurt were up to a third more expensive. The Food Commission accused manufacturers of cashing in on people's health concerns. Manufacturers said they charge more because only a few people want to buy such products. However, where prices are comparable – for example with reduced-fat milks – sales have soared. Sales of skimmed and semi-skimmed milk have now overtaken sales of full-fat milk.

MISLEADING FAT CLAIMS

The big letters on the front of the pack say 'low-fat', but should you believe it? Not necessarily. That's because low-fat claims can be selective and misleading. The problem is the law – or rather the lack of it, which makes it easier for companies to give a healthier impression of their product than it genuinely warrants.

In 1991 we were promised tough new regulations on health claims like 'low-fat' by the Ministry of Agriculture, Fisheries and Food (MAFF), but we're still waiting. It was proposed that **low fat** should mean less than 5 per cent fat by weight and less than 5 g of fat in a typical serving. **Reduced fat** should mean that the total fat content is less than three-quarters that of similar products that make no such claims. **Fat free** should mean less than one-sixth of 1 per cent fat. And the use of the word **very** – as in very-low-fat yoghurt – would not be permitted. But the proposals were not liked by manufacturers, many of whose products would no longer be able to make a low-fat claim, and MAFF and the European Commission went cold on the idea, leaving it possible for manufacturers to continue to mislead shoppers with unregulated claims.

Even more confusing is the use of the word **lite** or **light,** which has no clear meaning at all. Some manufacturers use it to mean reduced fat, but for other foods it may refer to reduced calories, salt, sugar, even alcohol. Other manufacturers use it to describe the colour or texture of a food! It's a meaningless term which should be outlawed, unless clearly defined.

Watch Out For

- foods claiming to be 'low' and 'reduced fat' which are in fact high-fat foods. For example 'low' and 'reduced fat' spreads typically contain 20–40 per cent fat. That's maybe less fat than in regular margarine or butter, but still makes for a high-fat food.
- claims such as '85 per cent fat free'. This isn't a low-fat food – there's 15 per cent fat, which is a fairly high percentage.
- 'low-fat' in big letters on the front of the pack. It may also be high in sugar, high in salt and low in fibre, but you won't find that emblazoned on the front.
- 'light' and 'extra light' claims – there's no standardised definition for these.

Sugar

Health experts recommend that we eat foods which are high in added sugar less often. Sugar can cause tooth decay, particularly in children and the elderly. In addition it provides 'empty' calories – that is, it provides no nutrients or vitamins, only calories (energy). Filling up on sugary foods mean less room for more nutritious foods – which may be a problem for those who don't eat a lot to start with, such as young children, slimmers and some older people. Sugar can often disguise high levels of fat in processed foods. Yet it's often impossible to tell how much sugar is in foods and drinks.

Sugar comes in many forms and some are worse for our health than others. For health it's important to distinguish between **intrinsic** sugars which are naturally locked into the structure of the foods in which they are found, as in fruits and vegetables. These are relatively harmless. **Extrinsic** sugars, on the other hand, have been added or are freely available in foods and can more easily damage teeth. Most sugar in processed foods is extrinsic. It's less important whether sugar is 'natural' or not. For example, the 'natural' sugar in an apple is intrinsic, but if processed to make juice it becomes extrinsic.

The sugar found in milk (lactose) is the one exception to this rule. Lactose is extrinsic but it is relatively harmless to teeth. That's why health experts talk about 'non-milk extrinsic' (NME) sugars as the ones we should cut down on.

To find out what type of sugar is in a given food you'll need to check the ingredients list.

How to Spot Hidden Sugars

Sugar may come in many disguises:

sucrose	maltose	maple syrup
invert sugar	hydrolysed starch	golden syrup
glucose	dextrose	honey
lactose	fructose	treacle
glucose syrup	brown sugar	fruit juices

Source: Health Education Authority, Scientific basis for dental health education, 4th edition, 1996.

SUGAR CLAIMS

The pack says 'no added sugar' but is it 'sugar-free'? Not necessarily. The group Action and Information on Sugars (AIS), in a review of over 1,400 foods making sugar-related claims, has criticised food companies of 'slippery and cunning' claims about the sugar content of their products.[3] AIS found:

- a third of products claiming to be sugar-free actually contained significant amounts of sugar – as much as 26 per cent sugar in the case of one instant custard.

- nearly 300 products claimed to be 'unsweetened' or to have 'no added sugar' but the ingredients included sugar-rich fruit syrups and juices
- a large number of products made claims about sugar but failed to declare their sugar content as required by law.

Sweet Nothings

'no added sugar' – Many people expect this to mean 'no added sugars of any kind', but this is not the case. Most manufacturers use it to mean 'no added sucrose' – that's ordinary sugar – and may well add all kinds of other sugars which are just as sweet and just as damaging to teeth. Watch out for 'no added sugar' foods sweetened with honey, syrups or fruit juices (sometimes concentrated).

'low-sugar' – there's no legal definition of 'low-sugar'. Guidelines say there should be less than 5 per cent by weight and less than 5g in a serving, but surveys have found products containing more and still calling themselves low-sugar, such as so-called 'low-sugar' rusks with 19 per cent sugar (about the same as a jam doughnut).

'sugar-free' – even sugar-free drinks are allowed to contain up to 0.5 per cent sugar, but in most cases the sweet taste of sugar-free drinks comes from artificial sweeteners. Parents often think that sugar-free drinks are harmless to children's teeth, but this is not the case – the acidity of fruit juices and low-calorie/sugar-free drinks can cause tooth erosion, damaging the tooth's enamel.

'unsweetened' – except, that is, for the sugars that are found naturally in the food (such as in 'unsweetened' fruit juice).

'reduced sugar' – again there's no law defining this, but guidelines say it should contain at least 25 per cent less sugar than a comparable product – a woolly definition at best.

'virtually sugar-free' – a meaningless term.

'less than X per cent added sugar' – this claim sounds healthy – you might even think the food was 'low' or 'reduced sugar' – but there's no guarantee that it is.

'high in carbohydrates' — this too sounds healthy but could mean it's got a fair amount of sugar. Carbohydrates include both complex carbohydrates (found in starchy foods such as pasta, rice, potatoes and bread, which we should eat more of) and simple carbohydrates (sugars). You need to check the ingredients list and nutritional information to see exactly what you're getting.

'lite'/'light' – it might mean less sugar, but there again it might not.

Not So Soft

It's often impossible to tell how much sugar is in a can of cola or a glass of orange squash. That's because many soft drink companies, including some of the most well-known brands, refuse to tell consumers about the high level of sugars in their drinks. Some products provide no nutritional information at all, while others just declare a figure for carbohydrate content but fail to reveal that this is almost entirely sugar. Some cans of cola or lemonade can contain up to ten lumps of sugar – well over half the recommended daily maximum of 60 g.

SUGAR ALTERNATIVES

There are two types of non-sugar sweeteners: bulk and intense sweeteners.

Bulk Sweeteners

These are used mainly to add both sweetness and bulk to food such as 'tooth-friendly', 'sugar-free' and 'diabetic' confectionery. They include:

hydrogenated glucose syrup   lactitol
sorbitol   xylitol
mannitol   maltitol
isomalt

Intense Sweeteners

These are added in small amounts, typically to 'diet', 'low-calorie' and 'lite' drinks and foods, though they are also used increasingly in non-diet foods alongside sugar. Questions remain over the safety of some artificial sweeteners (*see 'Additives', page 38*). Permitted artificial sweeteners are:

saccharin	acesulfame K
aspartame (trade name NutraSweet)	cyclamates
thaumatin	

Salt

Cutting down on salt could save 70,000 deaths a year from strokes and heart disease, according to leading public health researchers.[4] Health advisors recommend we cut our salt consumption by a third – from the present average of 9 g a day to 6 g – about two level teaspoonsful.

But, unlike advice to reduce our fat consumption, advice on cutting back on salt doesn't have official Department of Health backing. Salt, it seems, has become a political subject and hence an unmentionable four-letter word in official circles. In 1994, the Chief Medical Official at the Department of Health surprised many by refusing to endorse the advice of his expert scientific committee on cardiovascular disease: that companies should be urged to cut the salt in processed foods.[5] In addition, the Government prohibited discussions about salt in its Nutrition Task Force – the body set up to find practical ways of improving our nutritional health, and it declined to publish the sources of salt in its most recent survey on young children's diets. So what makes salt so sensitive?

It seems the manufacturers of processed foods don't much like this attention on one of their favourite ingredients. About 70 per cent of the salt we eat is already added to processed foods – only 15 per cent is added by us when we cook or at the table – so it's easy to see where the greatest reductions could be made. In fact, the Food and Drink Federation – the trade association which represents food manufacturers – went as far as threatening to pull out of co-operation with the Government over its Health of the Nation programmes unless the Government dissociated itself from the salt-reduction recommendations. And it seems they got their way when the Chief Medical Officer said it was not agreed Government policy that manufacturers needed to reduce salt levels in their products.

The food industry's rearguard action has not gone unnoticed, however. In 1996 the prestigious *British Medical Journal* entered the fray, strongly attacking the food industry for their attempts to stop Government from recommending salt reduction: 'Rather than reformulate their products, manufacturers have lobbied governments, refused to co-operate with expert working parties, encouraged mis-information campaigns and tried to discredit the evidence.'[6]

HOW MUCH IS TOO MUCH?

It can often be hard to work out how much salt you are actually eating. Not all products tell you how much salt is in them, while others give a figure for sodium content (this will include the sodium from salt as well as other ingredients such as monosodium glutamate or sodium bicarbonate). This can be confusing. It's recommended we eat no more than 6 g of salt a day – that's 2.4 g of sodium. To convert a sodium figure to salt content, simply multiply the sodium figure by 2.5.

Watch Out for Salt In:
- processed foods
- bread – a lot of salt in our diet comes from bread. This is not simply because bread is fairly salty – there's about half a gram per slice, but because we eat so much of it
- bacon, sausages, meat pies
- take-away foods
- breakfast cereals – even healthy-sounding ones can be high in salt

The Silent Killer

A high-salt diet, like the average UK diet, can be a cause of hypertension and high blood pressure which can lead to strokes, heart attacks and kidney failure. It's known as 'the silent killer' because it can strike without warning and many people are unaware that they may be at risk.

There may be other dangers from eating a salty diet. High salt intake has been linked to stomach cancer and asthma. There is also increasing evidence that a high-salt diet can lead to losses of calcium in the body, increasing bone thinning (osteoporosis). Thus, advice to increase the calcium in our diets, particularly for women, may be of little value if the amount of salt we eat is not reduced. Women of all ages are best advised to cut salt, not only to maximise bone mass while young but to prevent a high rate of loss when older.

SALT SUBSTITUTES

Treat salt substitutes with caution – they have no proven benefit and may still contain a substantial amount of salt. The best way to cut down on salt is to use only small amounts in cooking, avoid adding more at the table, eat less convenience and fast foods and look for low-salt versions of foods (but check the nutrition label – 'a little' is less than 0.1 g of sodium (*see 'Rule of Thumb Nutrition Guide', page 77*). Sea salt and iodised salt are not substitutes, though their stronger taste may mean you can use less. Try using more herbs and spices for different and more interesting flavours.

Fibre

The traditional British diet contains far too little fibre. Not only does this mean constipation and piles, but poses the risk of problems for the future. Eating more fibre can help to protect against heart disease, diabetes and some cancers.

Many people mistakenly believe that the way to increase fibre is to add raw bran to their regular foods. Bran is the outer coating of cereal grains like wheat, rice and maize which is often removed during processing. While it certainly provides plenty of fibre, it can also deprive the body of valuable minerals. That's because raw bran contains high levels of phytates – chemicals which bind with iron, zinc and calcium and prevent the body from absorbing these from food. Processed bran – found in wholemeal bread and high-fibre cereals – is less of a problem.

In fact there are different types of fibre and we should aim for a variety, including fibre-rich foods like pulses, fruit and veg and wholemeal bread and pasta. Some, such as that from wheat, is better at increasing the bulk of the faeces, while that in beans and some fruits is more effective in lowering cholesterol. We should aim for about 18 g of fibre a day.

TOP 10 FIBRE FOODS

Foods which provide about 5 g of dietary fibre include:

Shredded wheat	1 bowl
Wholemeal bread	2 slices
Baked beans	$^1/_3$ of a small (225-g) can
Frozen peas	1 tablespoon
Most vegetables	4–5 tablespoons
Boiled potatoes	2–3 large potatoes
Most fruits	6–7 oz (e.g. two small apples)
Dried figs and prunes	1 oz
Wholegrain rice	3 oz (uncooked)
Nuts	1–2 oz

CAN OAT BRAN LOWER CHOLESTEROL?

There's been a lot of debate over this one. Oats do contain a substance (called beta glucans and found in the soluble oat bran fibre) which is thought to lower cholesterol, but it's not clear how it works. What is clear is that you need to eat quite a lot – 100 g of oats (that's two bowls of porridge) every day for it to have any real effect. People with higher cholesterol levels are thought more likely to benefit.

Making Sense of Nutrition Labelling

If you really want to know how healthy the food you buy is, don't take too much notice of the claims and healthy-sounding words and symbols on the front of the packet – start reading the small print on the back. Nutrition labelling *should* make it easier to shop more healthily, but often doesn't.

Many foods now come with information on how much fat, protein, carbohydrate and energy is in the product. If you're lucky it might also tell you how much sugar, sodium (salt), saturated fat and fibre there is. But there's no law that says manufacturers must tell you. Only if manufacturers make a claim such as 'high in fibre' or 'low in fat' does the law say they must declare how much is there. The Government says that it wants companies to give nutrition information on their labels, but they are not prepared to pressurise the European Union to make it law.

Even when this type of information is there, it doesn't make a lot of sense to most people. It's as if companies decided on the most user-*un*friendly way of giving us information – though giving more useful information can in some cases actually be illegal. In one survey in which shoppers were shown standard nutrition labels, less than half had the slightest idea which foods were highest or lowest in sugar, fat and calories.[7]

Making it Simple

The Co-op food retailer has tried to help consumers make more sense of nutrition labels. The problem for most of us is that we've no way of knowing whether 3 g of fat is a lot, or whether 2.4 g of fibre is a good amount. In fact 1 g of fat per 100 g is low for fat but high for salt. So what the Co-op has done on its own-label products is add the

---

word 'high', 'medium' or 'low' alongside the grams of protein, fat, carbohydrates, sugar, fibre and sodium on the nutrition information panel. It's a simple and useful way of labelling, but in fact the Co-op could be breaking the law by helping consumers in this way. That's because European law only allows information to be given in standard formats (*see below*). Chances are no one will take them to court, but this illustrates the madness of a system that denies most shoppers a helpful way of making sense of nutrition labels.

If nutrition information is given then it must be presented in one of two ways. The most basic information provides data on only four nutrients (Basic Label):

- energy
- protein
- carbohydrate
- fat.

A fuller, more detailed list also gives information on:

- how much of the carbohydrate is sugar
- the amount of saturated fat in the total fat
- the amount of fibre
- how much sodium.

It might also provide figures for:

- the amount of monounsaturates and polyunsaturates in the fat
- starch
- cholesterol
- quantities of vitamins and minerals.

If a claim is made about a certain ingredient or nutrient, for example that it is 'low-fat' or 'reduced sugar', then the label must by law tell you how much of that ingredient or nutrient is in the product. But surveys have found that this information can be missing, making it impossible to assess the validity of the claim.

Information has to be given per 100 g or 100 ml. Information can also be given per serving or portion, in which case the label must indicate the weight or size of an average portion as well.

It all adds up to a lot of figures to read, but what does it all mean? It should be possible to use this information in a way that helps us to make healthier choices. But the problem is that the vast majority of us are not able to use this information in a useful way. And it's not our fault.

Telling us whether the amount is high, medium or low in words rather than numbers would be much more helpful. But manufacturers have staunchly resisted any attempts at making nutrition labelling mandatory, and to present the information in a more user-friendly way. So until the day this happens – if ever – here's a simple guide to demystifying nutrition labelling.

HOW TO READ NUTRITION LABELS

Energy
All foods provide energy but some are more energy-dense than others. Energy is measured in two ways on the label: in calories (written as kcal) and in joules (written as kJ). One kcal is roughly equivalent to 4 kJ. If you eat more energy than you require you'll put on weight.

Protein
The body uses protein for growth and repair. Most adults get more than they actually need.

Carbohydrate
Includes both complex carbohydrates (starches) and simple carbohydrates (sugars). Full labels tell you how much of the total carbohydrate is sugars. Nutrition labels which give only a single carbohydrate figure are not much help, as it's difficult to know

whether this means starch (we should eat more starchy foods) or sugar (which we may want to cut back on).

Sugars

Where information is provided this includes all sugars, both the sugars which occur naturally (intrinsic) and any added sugars. Most sugar in processed foods is added sugars, including fruit juices and honey (extrinsic sugars). These kinds of sugars can cause tooth decay and are mainly empty calories. Intrinsic sugars aren't normally a problem for teeth. To find out what type of sugar is in the food you'll need to check the ingredients list.

Fat

As mentioned earlier in this chapter, there are three main different types of fat: saturates, monounsaturates and polyunsaturates. We are advised to eat all fats sparingly and particularly to cut down on saturated fats.

Saturates

Eating too much saturated fat may raise your blood cholesterol and increase your risk of heart disease. Watch out for saturates in meat pies and sausages, etc., butter and cheese, and cakes and biscuits made with butter.

Twice as Fat

Each gram of fat provides 9 kcal of energy, while each gram of protein, carbohydrates (including sugar) and alcohol provides around 4 kcal of energy. That's why gram for gram (or ounce for ounce) fat is over twice as fattening as carbohydrate.

Fibre

Dietary fibre, or roughage as it used to be known, helps to keep the bowel healthy. It's better to get fibre from foods that contain it naturally, such as wholegrain cereals, fruits, vegetables and beans, rather than from added bran or other refined fibres.

Sodium

Most of the sodium in food is from common salt, but other additives or ingredients can add to sodium levels (e.g. monosodium glutamate). Sodium can raise blood pressure. More than two-thirds of the sodium we eat comes from processed foods.

HOW TO USE THE LABEL

You may be interested in different bits of information on the nutrition label. Slimmers, for example, may count calories, while people following medical advice to eat a low-salt diet may watch the sodium content of foods. And we're all advised to eat less fat, saturated fat, sodium and added sugar, and more fibre-rich foods. So how can you compare foods? How can you tell whether the figures mean foods are high or low in the nutrients you are interested in? How much is too much? And which nutrients are most important for health?

Tricky questions when you're faced with a table of numbers and are wondering whether you should have brought a calculator with you. But it's not as hard as it may at first seem to use the figures in a helpful way.

Comparing Foods

To choose between foods which you are likely to eat in roughly the same quantities: compare the amount of nutrient you get in 100 g. For foods which you eat in different amounts, compare the amount of nutrient you get in a serving or portion of each food.

How Much Is a Lot?

OK, you can read on the label that it's got 25 g of fat and 0.6 g of sodium per 100 g, but does that make it a high-fat food and a low-salt food? Twenty-five grammes of fat sounds a fair amount, and indeed it is, so you'd be getting a lot of fat. As for the sodium, 0.6 g sounds like very little but is in fact quite a lot.

The following table is a quick, handy guide to whether a food is high or low in a particular nutrient. You can use the figures as a rule of thumb for judging any food you buy. If it's a food where you eat the whole pack, like a ready meal or sandwich, compare the figure per serving given on the packet with the 'rule-of-thumb' guide below. For other foods, such as snacks or foods which you eat in relatively small amounts, look at the amount you get per 100 g.

Rule of Thumb Nutrition Guide

A **lot** means these amounts or more		A **little** means these amounts or less
10 g	**sugars**	2 g
20 g	**fat**	3 g
5 g	**saturates**	1 g
3 g	**fibre**	0.5 g
0.5 g	**sodium**	0.1 g

Source: 'Use your label: making sense of nutrition information' (MAFF, 1996).

Once you are used to judging what is a lot or a little, you can then work out whether figures that are in between are closer to being a 'lot' or a 'little'.

Adding It All Up

While you can now make rough judgements as to whether foods are high or low in particular nutrients, how can you tell whether, overall, you are eating enough fibre or too much saturated fat? Of course, by choosing more fibre-rich foods and less fatty foods you'll be on the right track. The following table will help you to see how foods fit into your whole diet. So, for example, you can work out how much of your daily fibre needs you will get from a bowl of breakfast cereal. Cornflakes, for example, with 0.3 g of fibre in an average bowl will give you less than 2 per cent of your daily fibre needs if you're a women – even less if you're a man. By contrast, two wholewheat breakfast 'biscuits' (such as Weetabix), with 4 g of fibre to a bowl, gives you between 20 and 25 per cent of your daily needs.

Similarly, if you eat a bar of chocolate containing 10 g of saturates, then you know that's half your recommended maximum daily intake, if you're a women, in just one snack. Or if you drink a can of lemonade or cola containing 6 g of sugar/100 g – that's nearly 20 g in a 330-ml can – you're getting nearly 40 per cent of your recommended maximum sugar intake from just that one can of drink.

Daily Guideline Intakes

		MEN	WOMEN
Fat	no more than	95 g	70 g
Saturates	no more than	30 g	20 g
Sodium	no more than	2.5 g	2 g
Fibre	at least	20 g	16 g
Sugar	no more than	70 g	50 g

Source: 'Use your label: making sense of nutrition information' (MAFF, 1996).

These figures have been produced by the Ministry of Agriculture, Fisheries and Food, based on average-sized men and women with average levels of physical activity. An average man needs about 2,500 kcal a day; an average woman about 2,000 kcal a day. Of course, in real life everyone is different and has different nutritional and energy needs. For example, a tall woman may need more than a small man; someone who is very active or has a physically demanding job may need more than someone who leads a very sedentary life. But as a general guide, such figures can be useful.

WHICH NUTRIENTS ARE MOST IMPORTANT?

Are some nutrients more important than others? If you are following a special medical diet, such as a low-sodium diet, then you'll be looking out specially for sodium figures. But even for those of us who just want to follow a reasonably healthy diet, some nutrients are indeed more important than others.

The most important nutrients are the amount of fat and saturates in food. Choose foods with the least fat, particularly the least saturates. Use only sparingly foods which are very high in fat, like butters, spreads, oils and creamy foods. And make certain you balance them with other foods which contain less fat.

Next check the sodium content. The less sodium, the better. Then check the fibre and the sugar. If you eat more calories than you burn up you will put on weight, so you may want to check the calories, but healthy eating doesn't mean avoiding calories or having to count calories all the time. If the food only comes with the Basic Label (*see page 73*), then the most important is fat.

WHAT ABOUT CHILDREN AND OTHER AGE GROUPS?

These guidelines apply to everyone over the age of five. For infants and children under two, sugar and sodium are the main nutrients to check. The amount of fat and fibre is not so important because children of this age have much smaller stomachs and there is a risk that a low-fat/high-fibre diet could fill them up without providing enough calories. From two years of age children should gradually move towards the same types of foods as adults. Children, teenagers and the elderly are particularly vulnerable to tooth decay, so they need to take more care over sugar and brushing their teeth.

Nutrition and Health Claims

These days health sells. New healthier-sounding foods are being launched virtually every week and manufacturers are busy relaunching existing products to tempt us into believing that they are good for us. Packs now come emblazoned with claims such as 'no added sugar' or 'low-fat', or boast added vitamins or other mysterious sounding ingredients that offer to protect us against heart disease, help our digestion or even enhance our moods. Heart-shaped logos and symbols and even endorsements from health charities add to the healthful hype. And many supermarkets have their own 'healthy eating' logos. Companies know that we're much more likely to pick healthy-sounding products off the supermarket shelves. But do these foods offer real benefits for our health? And how can we judge the products with genuine benefits from those that are pure marketing exaggerations?

The first thing to remember when it comes to claims about healthy food, is that there are very few laws regulating what manufacturers can say. Many people believe that nutrition and health claims are regulated. But, with a few exceptions, they are not. Treat all such claims with caution. Not only are there no legal definitions for many nutrition claims, but they can be used selectively to disguise a product's shortcomings. For example, a 'reduced fat' food may also be higher in salt or sugar; the label sometimes won't give you enough information to check this. It's best to treat such claims with care and use the Rule of Thumb guide (*page 77*) to help you make up your mind.

Many foods making a claim may be no better than other foods, for example breakfast cereals which claim they are 'low in fat'. Typically all breakfast cereals are low in fat, but they may also be high in sugar or salt, and many are much lower in fibre than you would expect.

Health-related Claims and the Law

The law currently governing claims relating to the healthiness of a food is inadequate. Claims are covered only by general legislation which states that they should not be misleading. This leaves too much leeway for spurious and selective claims. Consumer organisations and responsible manufacturers say they want clear rules to protect shoppers and reputable products.

General claims (e.g. full of goodness, wholesome, healthy, natural) – these are meaningless without further explanation.

Nutritional claims (e.g. 'low-fat', 'reduced salt', 'sugar-free', 'a good source of fibre') – there are no legal definitions for most of these type of claims, nor any rules covering how and when they can be used.

Health claims (e.g. 'can help lower cholesterol', 'for a healthy heart', 'an aid to digestion', etc.) – unregulated. Some health claims imply medicinal benefits.

Medicinal claims (e.g. that a product can help to prevent, treat or even cure a disease) – by law such claims are permitted only for products that are licensed as medicines. Not permitted for foods, though some dietary supplements (vitamins and minerals) may qualify.

FUNCTIONAL FOODS – HEALTH OR HYPE?

In the last couple of years a whole range of new foods alleging added health benefits have appeared on supermarket shelves. These so-called 'functional foods' make a virtue, not of cutting out ingredients like fat or sugar, but of *adding* supposedly beneficial ingredients which are then claimed to be good for the heart, to help digestion, to lower cholesterol and even to pep up your mind. On the face of it they sound a great step forward for nutritional health, but in reality many such claims are largely a marketing scam (*see 'Claims Explained', page 83*).

The National Consumer Council (NCC) is just one consumer organisation that has investigated the truth behind some of these claims.[8] The NCC's market research found that we are often confused and misled by the technical jargon manufacturers use to blind us with science. Health claims on food packs are more of a hindrance than a help; they make little sense to shoppers and so don't help them make healthy choices, the NCC concluded.

Yet most people believe that health claims such as 'helps maintain a healthy heart' or 'can actively improve your digestion' are officially controlled and monitored in some way. They are not, and this has allowed too many manufacturers to get away with making exaggerated and unsubstantiated claims. A number of newly launched products have been criticised by the Advertising Standards Authority for making unsubstantiated, misleading or exaggerated claims. But this rap over the knuckles from the ASA, coming long after the adverts have appeared and accompanied by no legal sanctions, is a poor substitute for proper regulation.

Many consumer organisations say health claims like these should be banned unless they can be properly regulated. In the US and other countries there are strict rules about the kinds of claims that manufacturers can make and the foods they can be made about. But in the UK health claims have become a virtual free-for-all, to the detriment of both consumers and honest food companies.

The Government has asked its Food Advisory Committee to make proposals for controlling health claims. The proposals state that claims should be properly substantiated with good evidence that the products can do what they claim. There are still no plans, however, to allow for claims to be approved before products are put on sale, or for the rules to be backed by the force of law.

Functional Junk

In a 1996 survey of over 700 food products claiming enhanced health or added nutritional benefits, the Food Commission found the majority to be foods of poor nutritional quality whose main justification was the added 'functional' ingredient.[9] The Food Commission

---

concluded that the vast majority of such foods, far from encouraging healthier diets, work directly against the efforts of the Department of Health to encourage a healthier diet through a better nutritional balance of foods.

Most claims are based on the fallacy that an added ingredient will be beneficial because foods which contain it naturally are considered to be beneficial. The survey found nearly 200 products – many high in fats and sugars – to which vitamins had been added; 47 products with added fibre, although expert advice is to eat a diet that has fibre 'as a naturally occurring component' not as an added ingredient, and nearly 100 products claiming to be high in protein, although protein deficiency is virtually unknown in the UK.

Food Industry U-turn

For years the food industry has been telling us that there is no such thing as a 'good' or a 'bad' food, in response to criticisms about foods of poor nutritional quality. What's important, they say, is the overall diet. Now, with functional foods, companies are falling over themselves to convince us that there are 'good' foods and that their latest designer product is the answer to your health needs. So what's the truth? Yes, it's true that your overall diet is important, but if you eat a lot of foods that are high in fat or salt it's going to be very difficult to balance these with other foods to achieve a varied, healthy diet overall.

Claims Explained

Cultural Revolution

Types of claims: *'helps maintain the balance of your digestive system', 'be alive with beneficial Bifidus and Acidophilus', 'can actively help to reduce blood cholesterol levels', 'helps to boost natural resistance'.*

So-called 'bio' yoghurts and yoghurt drinks come with added bacterial cultures – typically Bifidus and (Lactobacillus) acidophilus

– sometimes abbreviated to BA for the less microbiologically minded. Other products use more exotic strains. These bacteria exist naturally in our digestive system as part of the complex balance of microflora that maintains a healthy digestive and immune system. Our bodies need a healthy gut flora, but the jury is still out on whether eating these kinds of products can actually help. It's possible that in certain circumstances such products might top up depleted levels of bacteria in the gut, but there's no guarantee that they will. Tests have found some bio-yoghurts (and also some supplements claiming to contain 'gut-friendly' bacteria) were more dead than alive as they didn't contain enough bacteria to do any good. Even when they do contain reasonable levels, you'd probably need to eat them every day to get any benefits.

Verdict: There is insufficient evidence that these kinds of products can help *prevent* disease. Enjoy them if you like the taste.

Something Fishy

Types of claims: *'High in omega 3 ... which medical evidence suggests may have a role in helping prevent coronary heart disease'*, *'with added fish oil which may help maintain a healthy heart'*.

Fish oils, containing long-chain omega-3 fatty acids, have become the new miracle health product and now come as added extras in some spreads, cakes, bread and fortified health drinks. Putting aside the hype, there is some truth in this one (*see 'Good Fats', page 58*). We're advised to double our intake of long-chain omega-3 fats. There is good evidence that they can protect against heart disease and help with inflammatory diseases such as rheumatoid arthritis. Eating oily fish twice a week is one of the best ways to get recommended levels.

Products fortified with fish oils could help, but beware of exaggerated claims and check what else is in these products.

Verdict: Best to go for the oily fish.

Foods with Added Fibre

Types of claims: *'Soluble fibre ... can help reduce excess cholesterol, one of the risk factors of heart disease', 'enriched with fruit
and soluble fibre, nature's way of reducing cholesterol', 'can help
lower your cholesterol level'.*

Adding fibre to an unhealthy diet doesn't turn it into a healthy
one. Unfortunately some manufacturers have been trying to persuade us that it can by adding fibre to drinks and desserts. Official
health advice recommends we should get our dietary fibre from a
variety of foods which naturally contain fibre, rather than by products enriched with fibre.

**Verdict: Fibre-fortified products are an unrecommended
and expensive way to try and improve health.**

Foods with Added Vitamins

Types of claims: *'Now fortified with ACE vitamins, helping to protect your body from some of the harmful effects of today's stressful
lifestyles', 'with added vitamin C', 'vitamin enriched'.*

As evidence has emerged of the beneficial effects some vitamins
may play in helping to protect against diet-related diseases including heart disease and cancer, an increasing number of foods are
sold boasting added vitamins – from soft drinks, biscuits, canned
pasta and savoury snacks to ice lollies and even chewing gum.
Many are aimed at kids – or rather at parents, anxious that their little ones aren't eating enough greens. But, as with added fibre, it's a
mistake to believe that sprinkling a vitamin pill onto an otherwise
unhealthy diet will make it healthy. There's also the risk of distort-
ing the nutrient balance of the diet.

**Verdict: Watch out for other ingredients such as high lev-
els of sugar, fat and salt in fortified products.**

Isotonic sports drinks

Types of claims: *'helps fight dehydration and fatigue', 'gets to your
thirst – fast'.*

Isotonic means that the drink is at the same concentration as blood plasma, helping fluid to pass from the stomach to the blood more quickly. That's great if you're a serious sportsperson and need a quick burst of fluid or energy, but for most of us, so-called 'sports drinks' offer little benefit. You can get the same effect by diluting one part fruit juice with two parts water and adding a small pinch of table salt.

Verdict: Over-hyped.

Mood food

Types of claims: *'Revitalise your body and mind', 'stamina enhancer', 'enliven your spirits'.*

There's a whole range of soft drinks with a 'healthy' image that contain a range of weird and wonderful-sounding ingredients including taurine (an amino acid) and herbs such as ginseng, guarana, gingko biloba, schizandra and prickly ash bark. Many drinks offer to 'pep-u-up, revitalise, energise and rejuvenate'; others claim to 'soothe and enhance'. But there's nothing healthy about the high levels of sugar most contain. You're more likely to get a buzz from the caffeine in many brands than from any other ingredient.

Verdict: No more stimulating than a cup of sweet tea or coffee.

BANNED IN THE USA

Unlike the UK, the US has faced up to the problem of how to regulate health and nutrition claims. Their strict regulations define terms such as *low* (as in 'low-fat' or 'low-calorie'); *reduced* and *light*. In addition, the US rules permit only a limited number of health claims linking nutrients to disease prevention.

The following shows which nutrients can be linked to preventing and/or reducing the risk of certain diseases:

foods rich in calcium | osteoporosis in certain target groups (e.g. young women)

low-fat foods	reduction of cancer risk
low-saturated fat and low-cholesterol foods	coronary heart disease
fibre-containing grain products, fruits and vegetables	cancer and coronary heart disease
fruits and vegetables rich in vitamins A and C	cancer
low salt (sodium)	high blood pressure
folic acid-rich foods	birth defects such as spina bifida
oats	prevents raised cholesterol levels

Importantly, in the US no food can make a health claim if it is high in fat or salt, and there are restrictions on the use of health claims on other 'junk' foods such as sweets and soft drinks. Also, unlike in the UK, nutrition labelling is mandatory on virtually all packaged foods.

Dietary Supplements

It's not just foods that are making health claims. There's now a huge range of dietary supplements from simple vitamins and minerals to fish oils, amino acids, garlic, herbs and a whole host of other ingredients promising health benefits.

Each year we spend about £300 million on pills and potions, hoping to improve our health. But a survey of products by the Food Commission has found that many are making over-the-top claims; some could even be dangerous.[10] Consumer organisations say there should be better regulation of the dietary supplements market, with a system of pre-market approval of products and claims, and for there to be warnings for nutrients and ingredients where high levels may be a risk to health.

Dietary supplements fall into a grey area of regulation. Even though most people think of them as being more like medicines than foods, unlicensed dietary supplements fall under food legislation. Unlike medicines, which have to be proven effective and safe, supplements don't have to be tested for safety, there's no requirement for quality assessment (even though tests have found that some products don't contain what they claim to), and there's no prior approval of labels and health claims.

By law unlicensed products aren't allowed to make an explicit or implied 'medicinal claim' about what the product is for or what it can do, such as 'can help to prevent heart disease'. Some companies flout this rule, while others quite legally make similar-sounding 'health claims', either on packs or in promotional literature, such as 'can help to maintain a healthy heart'. The difference is so subtle that most of us are unlikely to perceive it. But it could mean a big difference in products. On the one hand a product with no clinical evidence that the product itself is good for you, on the other a medicinal product which is safe and pure and can prove it is clinically effective.

It's easy to see how consumers could be misled and confused, and how confidence in products which are genuinely beneficial could be undermined.

Folic Acid and Pregnant Women

There's now good evidence that the risk of having a baby with neural tube defects such as spina bifida can be reduced by ensuring that women have enough folic acid in their diet. Pregnant women, and women planning a pregnancy, are now advised to up their folic acid intake by eating more folate-rich foods such as oranges and green vegetables, folic acid-fortified foods such as breads, breakfast cereals and yeast extract, and by taking a daily 400 µg (microgram) folic acid supplement.

But as the law stands, products are not allowed to state the benefits of folic acid on products – that's a medicinal claim. The Co-op's decision to flout this law and make explicit the link between increased folic acid intake and the reduced risk of spina bifida, highlights the need for more sensible legislation which allows scientifically proven claims but outlaws rogue ones.

Meanwhile, the Health Education Authority has launched a folic acid-labelling 'flash' to enable women to identify foods fortified with folic acid.

Because of the lack of regulation, dietary supplements are making unsubstantiated health claims and getting away with it. In the last few years there have been a number of complaints to the Advertising Standards Authority about these kinds of products. The ASA is not a prosecuting body but it monitors advertising for its honesty and decency and can assess the evidence in support of claims to judge whether they are justified. The problem is that ASA rulings have no legal backing, and typically come months after adverts have appeared and promotional literature has been available.

Garlic Is Good for You, Is It?

'Avoid heart disease' says one leading brand of garlic supplements on the front of its pack. Together with its heart-shaped designs, the company gives the impression that their product can prevent heart disease. Such 'medicinal' claims should be made only if the product has a licence from the Medicines Control Agency. In this case, it hasn't. And when the Food Commission approached the company to ask for copies of the published research on which their claims were based, it was refused. 'If we released this information you might think we were making a medicinal claim. And that would be illegal,' a spokeswoman told the Food Commission.

Supplementary Warning

Some people like to take 'megadoses' of supplements. But with some vitamins there may be a risk from taking too much.

The Government has warned that prolonged intake of high levels of supplements containing vitamin B_6 could cause nerve damage, and now advises a daily intake of no more than 10 mg. But many of the commonly available supplements analysed by the Consumers' Association exceeded this limit in their recommended daily doses – some by as much as 25 times.[11] Most people can get all the B_6 they need from foods such as meat, fish, whole cereals and some vegetables. Meanwhile, the Government has announced that supplements with more than 10 mg will be available only on prescription.

Pregnant women should avoid supplements containing vitamin A – too much can be harmful to the developing baby. Beta-carotene has also raised concerns after studies found that men who took beta-carotene supplements were more, rather than less, likely to develop heart disease and lung cancer.[12] And in Australia, royal jelly must be labelled with a warning for people with asthma and allergies.

DO YOU NEED VITAMIN SUPPLEMENTS?

It's surprising but true, that those people who may least need dietary supplements take the most. Using data from the government's Adult Nutrition Survey it's possible to compare the vitamin intakes of people who take supplements compared with those who don't. What this shows is that, even after excluding the content of the supplement itself, those who take vitamin supplements have a higher intake of vitamins than those who don't.

This mean that, even without the supplements, the sorts of people who take supplements are already eating a diet with more vitamins in it than people who do not take supplements. And the figures show that both groups were getting well above the amount that the Government says they require.

It's possible to conclude from research like this that the people who buy supplements generally don't need them and that the effectiveness of supplements for the population at large may be of limited value. There is a counter-argument which says that recommended intake levels are set too low – at a level which merely prevents nutritional deficiencies – and that we may benefit from increased 'optimal' levels for health. The jury is still out on this one.

It's possible that in future we will understand more about the interactions and nutritional complexities of nutrients. Our understanding of the role of nutrients such as vitamins and minerals has taken great leaps forward in the last few decades. But, despite the scientific jargon and claims made for products, there is much that is not known about the effect of isolating particular nutrients and taking them as supplements. We cannot be confident that synthesising one particular form of a nutrient and adding it to our diet in large quantities will have the effect we hope for. It is far more likely that good nutrition and health are dependent upon complex interactions of nutrients – which are best supplied, not by expensive quick fixes in pills, but by real food. Some groups of people such as pregnant women, the elderly, some vegetarians, vegans or people with specific medical dietary requirements may require supplements, but these are generally the exception rather than the rule. It's sensible to get advice from a state registered dietitian, doctor, health visitor or other health professional before embarking on a course of self-medication.

Eating Vegetarian – Is it Healthier?

More and more people are becoming vegetarian (latest estimates put it at about 1 in 20 Britons). Concern about animal welfare is the main reason given for giving up meat, but many also believe it's healthier. And there is evidence to support this belief. Studies show that non-meat eaters tend to live longer and suffer less heart disease and cancer than meat eaters. But it's unclear whether vegetarians' healthier eating overall, rather than the lack of meat in their diet, provides the benefits. Vegetarians tend to eat more fruit and veg and are more health-conscious generally.

There's a worry that many teenage girls who become vegetarian are at risk of becoming anaemic. While a healthy, varied vegetarian diet can provide enough iron and calcium, it's not always easy to persuade youngsters of the benefits of eating their greens. Vegans, in particular, need to take care to ensure that they get enough vitamin B_{12} *(see pages 104–105)*.

Food for Babies
and Children

What parents don't want to do the right thing by their kids? Giving our children a healthy diet comes near the top of many parents' concerns. According to market research company Mintel, 83 per cent of mothers say they 'try to ensure their children eat a healthy diet'.[1] Parents from all social classes say it's the most important thing they consider when buying food for their children.

That's great news for the well-being of future generations, but too many kids are still eating diets that are shockingly poor nutritionally. So what's going wrong?

Chocolate and Chips

What are kids really eating? That's what one survey of 400 7- to 11-year-olds from different areas and backgrounds set out to discover.[2] The results were far from reassuring. Eight-year-old Christopher's diet for a day was fairly typical: toast, crisps, lemonade, sausage roll, doughnut, cola, two white rolls, chips and juice. Overall,

- most children ate a packet of crisps a day, and nearly all consumed sweets and fizzy drinks daily;
- chips were children's favourite food, with fruit and vegetables virtually absent;
- almost 40 per cent of the children's energy came from fat, found in popular high-fat foods such as ice cream, chips, crisps, sausages and beefburgers (the recommended amount is no more than 35 per cent);
- nearly a quarter of their energy came from sugar – about twice the recommended amount – mainly from eating sweets, fizzy drinks and foods with added sugars;
- many children were not getting enough vitamins and minerals including calcium, iron and vitamins A, C and E.

These results echo findings from other surveys which have found that children's diets are putting their health at risk.

The Young Wannahaves – Kids as Customers

Children are big business and have become an important market for companies selling food. Not only do children have their own pocket money to spend, they also have a considerable influence over what goes into the family shopping trolley. And the easiest way for companies to get their message to children is via the television. In the five years to 1996 the amount spent on advertising children's food doubled to reach £16 million, and it's still growing. According to one study, children in the UK are bombarded with more television adverts than their European counterparts.[3] And kids are never too young. One company appealed to the very young with its slogan 'chocolate for beginners'.

It's not just the adverts on TV and in kids' magazines that are out to persuade. There's a host of other marketing techniques which are honing in on your kids, including:

- cartoon and other popular characters adorning packaging and even the food itself (e.g. Barbie or Thomas the Tank Engine pasta); linking food products to movie characters or toys.
- celebrity endorsements from sports and pop stars.
- TV sponsorship. As well as adverts between the programmes the programmes themselves can now be sponsored by companies.
- free give-aways, things to collect and competitions on food packets (e.g. breakfast cereals and McDonald's Happy Meals), which help to fuel children's 'pester power' to persuade their parents to buy the product, time and time again.
- products given away through schools. These come with the apparent endorsement of authority figures (that is, teachers). According to the National Consumer Council, much so-called free educational material sent to schools by companies is biased and plastered with company logos, or actively encourages children to eat chocolate and fast food.[4]
- commercial Internet sites can collect information about children which can then be used to sell products to them.
- sponsored children's clubs and sponsorship of children's sports and cultural events associate a company's name and products with enjoyable activities.

With such promotions on the increase, many are asking whether aggressive marketing to children and teenagers is socially responsible. Alcopop manufacturers have caused widespread concern with their cynical attempts to woo young drinkers with alcohol dressed up as soft drinks. There was an outcry when plans, apparently endorsed by the Department of Education, were unveiled for schools to display advertisements in return for cash. Now snack food companies are offering youngsters the chance to win thousands of pounds in promotions. Some say that these promotions break the spirit (if not the letter) of the rules preventing children from gambling.

Cashing in on Kids

Children under 16 can't buy lottery tickets or scratch cards, but a loophole in the law means that food companies can encourage children into underage gambling, and it's all quite legal. Top-selling brands of crisps, sweets and soft drinks have jumped on the 'lottery fever' bandwagon and are cynically boosting sales by offering youngsters the chance to win thousands of pounds with scratch cards, lucky wrappers or instant-win coupons.

Companies can get away with it because they are selling the product, not the scratch card. And it's turned out to be good business – youngsters told one TV programme they bought the snacks, even if they didn't like them, in the hope of winning cash prizes.

A DIET OF JUNK FOOD ADVERTISING

British children are exposed to the most food advertising in Europe, and the majority of products encourage poor eating habits. These were the findings of an international comparison of advertising during children's programmes carried out by Consumers International.[5] This and other surveys carried out in the UK show that food advertising during programmes for kids is dominated by adverts for foods that do little to encourage a healthy diet, such as confectionery, sweetened cereals, soft drinks, savoury snacks and fast food. Consumers International found a staggering 95 per cent of UK adverts monitored were for foods that encourage a fatty, sugary, salty diet. Sixty-two per cent of adverts were for foods high in fat; 50 per cent for foods high in sugar, and 61 per cent for foods high in salt. The survey found only a handful of advertisements for healthier foods.

The most prolific advertiser in the international survey was McDonald's: commercials for the fast food chain were found in virtually every country. In 1997 the High Court ruled, in the libel trial brought by McDonald's, that the company's advertising and marketing did 'make use of susceptible young children to bring in custom, both their own and that of their parents who must accompany them, by pestering their parents.'[6]

Furthermore, the judge ruled that the fast food chain's 'advertising, promotions and booklets have pretended to a positive nutritional benefit which McDonald's food, high in fat and saturated fat and animal products and sodium, and at one time low in fibre, did not match.' With one Australian study finding that just over half of 9- and 10-year-olds think that Ronald McDonald knows best what is good for children to eat, it's hardly surprising that children can get a distorted view of health and nutrition from food advertising. With advertising making food that is less healthy actually seem more attractive and desirable, it's little wonder that health messages are undermined and meal times are often a battle ground.

WHAT OTHER COUNTRIES DO

In the UK, TV adverts must conform to standards laid down by the Independent Television Commission (ITC) but there are no restrictions, beyond those that apply to all advertising, on the amount of advertising that can be aimed at children. Other countries do things differently.

- Sweden and Norway do not allow any advertising to children under 12, and no advertisements at all are allowed during children's programmes.
- Australia does not allow advertisements during programmes for pre-school children.
- Austria does not permit advertising during children's programmes. The Flemish region of Belgium also prohibits advertising five minutes before and after children's programmes.

Cybertots on the Net

A US study[7] of Internet advertising directed at children discovered unfair and deceptive forms of marketing which are outlawed in other media. The researchers found advertising and content seamlessly

---

interwoven in on-line 'infomercials' for children, who can spend hours playing with popular 'spokescharacters' such as Tony the Tiger, Chester Cheetah and Snap!, Crackle! and Pop!

Watching TV Makes Kids Fat

Watching TV can slow children's metabolism down to a level lower than when they are doing nothing at all, according to research published in the *American Journal of Paediatrics*. This finding – coupled with the fact that children who watch a lot of TV spend less time outside playing and using up energy, and more time having their taste buds teased by advertisements for high-fat, high-sugar snack foods – gives credence to the long-held belief that too much TV is bad for kids' health.

Food for Kids

You may be getting more than you think with some food for kids.

BREAKFAST CEREALS

A bowlful of cereal could be a healthy start to the day for youngsters, but you'll need to choose carefully. Many cereals made to appeal to children are packed full of sugar, many are high in salt and low in fibre, and any vitamins and minerals have largely been added. Some are little more than confectionery. With sugar accounting for up to half the weight of ingredients, some are twice as sweet as a jam doughnut. And with free collectibles, competitions and special offers on cereal packs, they are a prime target for children's 'pester power'.

Eating cereal for breakfast ensures children get milk, which is good for calcium and protein. But check the labels and choose cereals that are not sugar-coated and which are made from wholegrain cereals, such as Weetabix, Shredded Wheat and similar cereals. Even if your kids add a teaspoon of sugar at the table it will be a lot less than the four or five teaspoons that some cereals contain.

CEREAL BARS

It's easy to think cereal bars are a healthier alternative to sweets and biscuits, but are they? Researchers from Manchester University found that some popular brands contain more fat than a Mars bar, while others are sweeter than chocolate digestives. Beware of products laden with sugar in the form of raw cane sugar, honey, corn syrup, molasses or glucose syrup. And watch out for hydrogenated fat, which is just as unhealthy as saturated animal fats. Despite their image these bars are not necessarily good sources of fibre.

CRISPS AND SAVOURY SNACKS

Children now prefer a bag of crisps to an apple, a banana or a yoghurt, and the growing popularity of snacking is contributing to children's poor eating habits. In a survey of top-selling crisps and snack brands, the Food Commission[8] found:

- snacks containing a cocktail of additives (including flavour enhancers, antioxidants, artificial sweeteners, colours and flavours) all of which are banned in foods made specifically for babies and young children;
- savoury snacks to be as damaging to children's teeth as biscuits;
- manufacturers using unhealthy hydrogenated vegetable oils.

One professor of nutrition, paid by the snack and crisps manufacturers, claimed that crisps are nutritionally OK because they contain more vitamin C than an apple. But what he failed to say was that they are also high in fat and salt, and that apples are not a great source of vitamin C in the first place. Lower-fat crisps are a healthier alternative, but are still relatively high in fat.

FISH FINGERS

Most kids love fish fingers. They are a relatively cheap and attractive way to encourage reluctant fish eaters to eat a highly nutritious food. But be warned: you may be getting less fish for your money than you think. Less than half of some fish fingers are actually fish. You could be getting more coating and additives than you bargained for.

ICE CREAM

Soft ice cream is a popular summer favourite – and quite a feat of food technology. It was Mrs Thatcher who as a food technologist in the 1950s worked on pumping air into ice cream. And that's what you largely get today – a lot of air and water trapped in an emulsion of concentrated skimmed milk, hardened vegetable fat, sugar and a whole host of additives including emulsifiers, stabilisers, flavourings and colours. It's a long way from the traditional way of making ice cream with milk, cream, sugar and eggs.

SOFT DRINKS

Most soft drinks are packed with sugar. A can of cola, carton of juice drink or small bottle of fizzy pop typically contains some 30–40 g of sugar each – that's about 10–15 sugar cubes. Yet it's rare for major brands to inform consumers of their sugar content.

It's well known that sugar is bad for children's teeth; less well known is the damaging effects that many fizzy drinks – including sugar-free and 'diet' drinks as well as fruit juices – may have in causing dental erosion (damage to the enamel and dentine). Dentists are seeing more and more children with this problem.

We tend to believe that fruit juices are pure and natural and less likely to damage teeth, but the acidity in fruit juices can be just as damaging as sugar to teeth. For young children, water or milk is best; juices should be drunk diluted – one part juice with four to six parts water – and preferably limited to meal times. Greatest damage to teeth is done when drinks are sipped or drunk out of a feeding bottle over a long time (say, the course of a day). The damage can start within 45 seconds of consuming an acid drink and can continue for an hour. If you think having your children brush their teeth after they've had a sweet drink is the answer, then think again. Brushing the teeth at this time can actually *increase* the damage done, although brushing the teeth with a fluoride toothpaste shortly *before* drinking can help to reduce the damage.

SWEETS

Sweets have always been made attractive to children. But despite moves towards more natural colours, some products still contain artificial colours which can cause allergies and hyperactivity in a small number of children and which are banned in foods for babies and young children.

Tooth-friendly sweets offer a safer choice. But the alternative sweeteners used, such as sorbitol, can be laxative or cause digestive problems. Products must carry warnings advising not to eat too much.

YOGHURTS

Yoghurt and fromage frais are a good source of protein, calcium and some B vitamins. Yet despite their healthy image they can also come with a lot more besides – including added sugar, thickeners, colours and flavourings. Fruit syrups, purées and concentrates add to the sugar while providing little good nutrition. Some small pots of fromage frais can contain as much as nearly four sugar lumps' worth of non-milk sugars. With cartoon characters and colourful packaging, manufacturers make a point of appealing to children with these products. Even baby and toddler products typically come with higher sugar levels than if parents made their own with plain fromage frais blended with freshly puréed fruit. They may also come with additives banned in foods for babies and young children.

Junk with Added Vitamins

How do you turn junk food into a health food? Simple, throw in a crushed-up vitamin pill and market it as the latest way for parents to help their offspring eat more healthily. But such tricks are more of a supercon than superfood. It's not that difficult these days to find sweets, ice lollies, fizzy drinks and squashes, desserts and even crisps and other snacks with added vitamins. One manufacturer actually claimed that their crisps would 'help achieve a more balanced diet for the British public'.

However good such claims sound, the fact is that it's typically highly sweetened, fatty, processed foods that are trying to give themselves an aura of health. Manufacturers argue that children will eat sweets anyway so it's better that they eat sweets with added vitamins. But children need a wide range of vitamins and minerals, not just one small dose of added vitamin C, and the best way for them to get all they need is from real food that provides a healthy balance of nutrients.

Vitamins with Added Junk

Mothers are giving up the battle to make their kids eat their greens, say health campaigners. Cabbage and sprouts are top of the kids' hate list; broccoli, green beans and peas are also disliked. The problem, says the Cancer Research Campaign, which commissioned the research, is that a whole generation of children are growing up without the protection against cancer which fruit and vegetables provide. The CRC thinks the answer is to team up with the frozen food retailer Iceland to produce baked bean-flavoured peas, pizza-flavoured sweetcorn, chocolate-flavoured carrots, and cheese and onion-flavoured cauliflower. Others, though, are not convinced that drowning good veg in artificial flavours, all kinds of non-nutritious additives, artificial sweeteners, sugar and salt is the way to go.

Not So Clever

The media loved it – a whole documentary was devoted to it – it's the claim that vitamins can boost your child's IQ. But in 1992 the company at the heart of the controversy – Larkhall Natural Health Ltd – was fined £1,000 and £35,000 costs for claiming that its Tandem IQ vitamin pills for children could improve intelligence. The case, brought by Shropshire Trading Standards, held that the labelling was misleading in that it gave the impression that the pills could increase the IQ of most children regardless of their nutritional state. The court accepted that only children with a serious dietary deficiency were likely to benefit from supplements – no improvements in IQ could be demonstrated for children eating a reasonable diet.

GOING VEGGIE

Many parents worry that their children will be going short of essential nutrients when they announce their intentions to become vegetarian. However, eating a vegetarian diet can be just as healthy as a meat-based one, and can be a lot healthier, but only if you're eating a wide variety of foods including lots of fruit and vegetables, starchy carbohydrates such as pasta, rice, bread and potatoes as well as pulses and nuts. Too much reliance on processed foods, even if they are vegetarian, or too much cheese, which is very high in saturated fat, will not provide the same kind of health benefits.

So going veggie does need some careful planning and discussion with your children to ensure that they understand that being a vegetarian means more than just cutting out meat. It can also be the opportunity to consider the kinds of food the whole family eats – not so everyone has to become a fully paid-up member of the Vegetarian Society, but to introduce more meals based around fresh vegetables and fruits, starchy, wholegrain foods, pulses and nuts. Cutting out meat means reducing the amount of saturated fat – but beware of eating too much saturated fat from hard cheeses or other high-fat dairy foods.

The results of one survey should provide some reassurance for parents.[9] This study of 50 vegetarian children aged between 7 and 11 found that they were eating more healthily than matched meat-eaters. They were eating more fibre and less saturated fat, although the researchers did find lower levels of iron in their blood. Many vegetarian foods are good sources of iron, but it's harder for the body to absorb iron from plant-based foods than from meat. Teenage girls, particularly those on slimming or vegetarian diets, may be at risk of low iron intakes. It's important to ensure that all teenage girls, not just vegetarians, include some good sources of iron in their diet every day, such as:

- wholemeal bread, pasta and brown rice
- some breakfast cereals are fortified with iron (choose low-sugar brands)
- pulses, including chickpeas and lentils
- eggs – the iron is in the yolk
- all kinds of nuts, sesame seeds and tahini (in hummus)
- dried fruits, especially apricots but also raisins, prunes, figs, dates
- potatoes, broccoli and other dark leafy vegetables are good sources of iron
- Vitamin C helps the absorption of iron, so drinking a glass of orange juice or other vitamin C rich drink with meals can help.

All the above foods, with the exception of eggs, are also good sources of calcium, which is important for growing teeth and bones and, for teenage girls, to protect against osteoporosis (bone loss) later in life.

Many parents also worry that vegetarian youngsters may be missing out on protein. However, cheese, dairy products, eggs, pulses, nuts and grains all contain protein; unless a child is eating a very restricted diet, protein deficiency is extremely rare.

Vegans

Vegans eat a much stricter diet than vegetarians, eating no animal products at all – that means no eggs, milk or other dairy products, and no honey. There are worries that vegans may not get enough iron, nor vitamin B_{12} which is found in meat and dairy foods. For this reason it's a good idea to include fortified breakfast cereals, margarine, yeast extract, textured vegetable proteins or fortified soya milks in the diet.

Meat Alternatives

The image of vegetarian food is a healthy one – but not all foods sold as meat alternatives live up to this. A Food Commission survey[10] of vegetarian sausages and burgers found that some were as fatty as regular meat sausages, while most contained unhealthy fats in the form of saturated fat or hydrogenated vegetable oils, which can be just as harmful as animal fats. With overall fat content ranging from 30 to 80 per cent of calories, you need to take a close look at the label to make a healthier choice.

Foods for Babies

THE RIGHT START

Despite the benefits of breastfeeding for both mother and baby, only two-thirds of women in the UK try it, and by four months only a quarter are continuing, far less than in many other countries. One of the reasons so few women start and continue with breastfeeding is the promotion of breastmilk substitutes. Baby milk companies in this country spend approximately £12 million on commercial promotion through the health care system, while less than £150,000 is spent by the Government on information about breastfeeding. In Norway, where there is no promotion of artificial feeding and much more support for breastfeeding mothers, 98 per cent of women leave hospital breastfeeding and 75 per cent are still breastfeeding at six months.

Baby Milk Blues

There's good evidence that the activities of baby milk companies are reducing the numbers of women breastfeeding worldwide. One recent report by organisations concerned with child health[11] highlights violations of the World Health Organization's International Code on the Marketing of Breastmilk Substitutes by companies, including leaflets given to mothers in shops, free samples given out in clinics, brand name gifts to health workers and the display of posters implying the superiority of formula milks to breastmilk. The study of women from Poland, Bangladesh, Thailand and South Africa found that between two to three times as many women who weren't exposed to company information or given free samples were breastfeeding, compared to those who were.

FORMULA MILKS

Formula milks can never fully match up to breastmilk. No breastmilk substitute contains the full range of nutritive factors and antibodies that breastmilk provides. Even in this country where clean and safe water is available, bottle-fed babies are 5–10 times more likely to suffer diarrhoea than breastfed infants. And some studies have shown that babies who are breastfed are more intelligent and have better visual development. It's thought this may be due in part to a particular fatty acid, known as DHA, which is found in breastmilk. Some formula milk manufacturers are now considering adding an artificially formulated DHA to their milks, some of which may be genetically engineered.

In recent years there have also been a number of 'scares' over the safety of baby milks, ranging from 'gender-bender' chemicals to salmonella food-poisoning bacteria. Despite the risks that newborn babies may face from possible chemical contaminants in baby milks, no maximum limits have been set. Only in 1995 did a European Directive say that maximum safety levels should be set *without delay* – but these won't come into force until 1999.

Phthalates in baby milk

In 1996 Government tests found low levels of chemicals known as phthalates in infant formula milks. Phthalates are chemicals that have long been used in plastics, though it's only relatively recently that it has been discovered that phthalates and other chemicals can mimic the female hormone, oestrogen. These hormone-disrupting chemicals have been linked to falling sperm counts in men, problems of sexual development and possibly some cancers (*see 'Gender-bender Chemicals', page 54*).

The Government analyses of formula milks found that all of the brands tested were contaminated with phthalates. Yet the Ministry of Agriculture, Fisheries and Food (MAFF) refused to name the brands, even though there was an eight-fold difference between the highest and the lowest levels found. MAFF and the Department of Health insisted that all fell well below safe levels, although they had to admit that these safety margins do not take into account phthalates' oestrogenic effects. Companies were asked to find out where the phthalates were coming from and to investigate ways of reducing levels, but were not given a deadline.

The Safety of Soya Formula for Babies

Most infant formulas are made from cows' milk that has been modified to make it suitable for babies. But for the small number of bottle-fed babies who are allergic to cows' milk, soya formula is usually suggested as an alternative. Now the safety of these formula milks is under question. That's because soya contains substances known as phytoestrogens – literally plant oestrogens. There's some evidence that for adults these may help protect against certain cancers, but for infants there's concern that they could interfere with natural hormones and affect development. Babies feeding exclusively on soya formula consume per kg of weight several times the amount of phytoestrogens which have been demonstrated to cause changes in the monthly cycles of women. And although research on humans is limited, phytoestrogens have been found to cause infertility and affect sexual development and behaviour in animals.

The Department of Health stressed that there is no evidence of harm to babies at this stage but that more research is urgently needed. As a precaution, soya formula companies have been asked to reduce the amount of phytoestrogens in their formulas – though companies say this might be difficult. The Chief Medical Officer advises that soya formula should only be given to babies on the advice of a doctor or other health professional. For parents concerned about their babies developing allergies, he stressed that breastfeeding is the best way to protect them. The DoH advises that it is OK for older children to drink regular soya milk because, by then, youngsters are eating a much more varied diet and milk is no longer their sole source of nutrition.

Not only does soya formula come laced with oestrogenic chemicals, it also has high levels of added sugar in the form of glucose which can rot teeth. It may also come as a surprise that soya itself can be an allergen.

FOLLOW-ON MILKS

Follow-on milks are sold for babies over six months with the promoted benefit of containing more iron. Certainly babies should not be given unmodified cows' milk as a drink until they are over one year old, mainly because of the possible risk that cows' milk may trigger allergic conditions such as asthma and eczema. But whether babies need follow-on milks is open to debate. The World Health Organization's view is that they are not necessary.

There is evidence that some older children aged between one and three may not be getting enough iron due to their poor diet. For babies under one, the best advice is ensure that the weaning foods you give are of good nutritional quality and that you either continue to breastfeed or give a formula milk. Over the age of one, the Department of Health advises you can give full-fat regular milk.

Reduced-fat milks should not be given to children under two and should only be given to children under five if they eat a good diet – it's best to check with a health visitor or doctor first. Very young children need a diet that is high in calories to meet their growth and energy needs. Over the age of five it's sensible to be careful about the amount of fat children are getting. Once they reach this age the majority of children are eating too much fat, and many are not getting enough exercise, which can lay the seeds of heart and health problems in later life.

BABY FOODS

Starting your baby on solid foods is an important step. Expert advice now warns against starting babies on solid food before the age of four months. It can be an anxious time, with parents often unsure which are the best foods for their babies. Reassuring words on labels and advertising make it easy for parents to think that commercial baby foods offer better quality and nutrition for their babies than the foods they might make at home. But too many tins, jars and packets of baby foods come with unwanted, unnecessary and poor quality ingredients.

What's in Commercial Baby Food?

- **sugar** – unnecessary sugars, including fruit juices and fruit concentrates, are often found in first foods (even savoury ones). The Food Commission[12] has found that over half of first-stage products contained non-milk extrinsic (NME) sugars. Sugar provides no nutrients apart from calories, encourages a sweet tooth and its use is condemned by experts as putting emerging teeth at risk. Government experts advise weaning foods and drinks should be *'free as far as possible from NME sugars'.*[13]
- **maltodextrin** – a bulking agent and highly refined starch which absorbs water easily to make an instant gluey paste used in many dried foods. Also used to stick envelopes and postage stamps. Pleasant-tasting but provides no useful nutrition apart from empty calories. May encourage tooth decay.

- **modified starch** – low-cost, low-nutrient thickener used to bulk out baby food; made from chemically treated cornflour. Other low-nutrient thickeners may be described on labels as modified cornflour, starch, wheatstarch. Although it's claimed that such starches are easy to digest, there is some evidence that modified starch may adversely affect babies' digestion, particularly in the presence of sugars.
- **dried skimmed milk powder** – added to boost protein levels cheaply; unsuitable for babies with allergies or a family history of them.
- **gluten** – found in most cereals, except oats, maize and rice. Not suitable in foods for babies under six months old. Can increase the risk of provoking coeliac disease.
- **added water** – used to reduce the quantity of 'real' food.
- **added vitamins and minerals** – added to replace nutrients lost during processing, or missing due to lack of nutritious ingredients. Reassures parents about the quality of products.
- **hydrolysed vegetable protein** – provides a meaty taste. Manufacturers have been quietly removing HVP from their products as there are questions over its safety for babies.

Baby food companies have come in for criticism for bulking out baby foods with starches, fillers and added water rather than using more 'real' ingredients. In 1997 over 60 per cent of more than 400 products examined by the Food Commission[14] were being bulked out with low-nutrient starches, a practice the Food Commission has described as providing babies with 'tinned paste' and 'polyfiller' meals at the expense of real nutritious ingredients.

EU legislation which one might hope would set higher standards has done nothing to improve the quality of such baby foods. Meals called 'lamb hot-pot' and 'turkey dinner' can legally contain as little as 10 per cent meat, with much of the rest made up of fillers and water.

To check what you are buying you'll need to read the label carefully and look for unnecessary starches and maltodextrin.

Genetically-altered Baby Foods

Most baby food companies say they will not be able to guarantee that soya ingredients in baby foods will be free from genetically-modified soya once their existing stocks of soya run out, according to a 1997 survey of companies by the Food Commission. However, buying organic baby food will ensure no gene-altered ingredients – organic food is not permitted to contain them.

Empty Phrases

It's not just poor quality ingredients that get the thumbs down. As companies vie for the tastes and tummies of tiny eaters, phrases on labels designed to reassure parents are under fire for being meaningless or misleading. Phrases such as *carefully developed ... specially formulated ... provide a balanced, highly nutritious diet ... properly balanced* can undermine parents' confidence in their own home-prepared foods.

Watch out too for pictures on the packet. One vegetable and chicken dinner examined by the Food Commission came with a picture of several slices of chicken on the packet, but actually contained less chicken than added maltodextrin starch. And a cheese, spinach and potato bake had cheese first in the title but eleventh in the ingredients list, with more low-nutrient maltodextrin than cheese.

Choosing Better Baby Foods

Making your own baby food ensures you know exactly what it contains. It's easier and less time-consuming than many new parents imagine, particularly if you have a blender or a baby mouli and a freezer to store food in small portions – an ice-cube tray is ideal. And it's cheaper, too.

When my daughter was ready for solids I decided that, as I didn't live on jars, tinned and packet food, there was no reason why she needed to. She was a great fan of my cooking and enjoyed a tremendous variety of tastes. When on occasion she was offered commercially prepared foods she often disliked them. I also found homecooking made it much easier to progress onto more lumpy foods as she grew older. This can sometimes be a difficult progression, but I could control the consistency of the food depending on her taste that day.

Some commercial baby food companies are now beginning to listen to parents' concerns and are offering baby foods made without starches, maltodextrin or other thickeners. Some use only organic ingredients, too, ensuring that they are free from pesticide residues. In 1989 the Government told baby food manufacturers to reduce pesticide levels in infant foods as much as possible, although they failed to set stricter standards for these levels, despite evidence that children may be at greater risk from their effects.

Alar in Apple Juice

It was the pesticide Alar which first made many parents aware of the possible risks from chemicals sprayed onto foods commonly eaten by babies and young children. In 1989 campaign groups estimated that one in a thousand children could develop cancer from the use of Alar. The chemical, used to control fruit ripening, could not be washed or peeled off the fruit and it was claimed that its active ingredient breaks down into a potent carcinogen when apples are cooked, processed or made into juice.

MAFF insisted that the risks were exaggerated and refused to ban the chemical. But sustained campaigning led the manufacturers of the pesticide to withdraw it.

BABY DRINKS

Despite expert advice that sweetened drinks are not advisable for babies, companies are cynically marketing highly sugared drinks for babies as young as a few months old. 'Baby' and 'toddler' juice drinks, often sold in individual cartons with a straw, are using claims of added vitamin C to disguise their less than desirable qualities. The Government's COMA committee report on Weaning and the Weaning Diet (1994) specifically recommended: 'Infants should be weaned onto foods and drinks free as far as possible of NME sugars' due to their potential harm to newly emerging teeth.

This committee also recommended that the sugar content of such drinks should be shown, but not all manufacturers do this – making it impossible for parents to know that they may be giving their children highly sugared drinks. Watch out for products claiming to be 'free from added sugar' when the product contains NME sugars from fruit juice which are just as damaging to teeth.

Add to this the problems of straws – dentists say straws encourage sweet fluids to remain in contact with teeth for longer, compared with drinking from a cup or glass – and these are not drinks to be recommended as a regular part of a young child's diet. Sweet drinks like these not only encourage a sweet tooth but may also dull a baby's appetite by filing him or her up with sweet calories. It's far preferable to offer water (previously boiled for babies) and milk.

Damage to Teeth

Tooth damage can happen even when sugar and juice are at low concentrations, and can occur even before teeth have emerged. If you do use these drinks don't give them regularly, use a beaker or cup (never a bottle) to minimise the time the drink is in the mouth, and give at meal times rather than between meals.

Some manufacturers have replaced sugar with maltodextrin, a soluble starch, in so-called 'low-sugar' drinks. But even this is thought to cause tooth decay and it will dull the appetite with non-nutritious calories.

Herbal Drinks

Herbal drinks are sold for babies as young as a few weeks. But Government experts are examining whether they are suitable for ones so young. They are worried that not enough is known about the effects of herbal extracts on newborn babies. Manufacturers say that the drinks contain so little herbal extract that it can't possibly have any effect. So why, one wonders, are they adding it at all? Presumably to disguise the sugar that the majority of these products also contain.

What's Wrong with Water?

Nearly three-quarters of pre-school children never drink water. That's the staggering statistic discovered by researchers from Southampton University.[15] The two- to five-years-old that they studied were drinking squash and fruit drinks (37 per cent of all drinks), milk (18 per cent), diet drinks (14 per cent) as well as tea and pure fruit juices. But barely one in ten was drinking water more than once a day. For children attending infant school the figures were slightly better – but still only one-third were drinking water more than once a day.

Not only were youngsters' teeth at risk from these other drinks but the researchers determined that many children may be suffering from 'squash drinking syndrome', with loss of appetite, poor weight gain and 'toddler diarrhoea'. Some pre-school children were estimated to be getting more than half of their daily calories from the sugar in soft drinks. Poor appetite and poor behaviour at meals, which some mothers described, were greatly reduced when the quantity of soft drinks was cut. Youngsters were so used to sweet drinks that they had to be weaned off them by gradually diluting the amount of sugar until they accepted water.

The researchers also criticised the way in which such drinks are promoted as healthy and the way in which manufacturers exploit a vulnerable population for their own benefit.

ARTIFICIAL SWEETENER OVERDOSE

Foods for babies and young children are not permitted to contain a range of additives, including artificial sweeteners, but a loophole in the law means that other foods including soft drinks, crisps and other snacks and ice lollies often contain artificial sweeteners, some as a double-sweet dose alongside sugar. There's a risk that it's all too easy for some young children to consume more than the amount considered safe of some artificial sweeteners.

Not Too Sweet

In 1990 the Food Advisory Committee became alarmed at children's consumption of one sweetener, saccharin. A staggering one in six (17 per cent) of under-fives were consuming more than the World Health Organization's recommended daily intake. They were getting most of it from soft drinks – and not the diet variety, but the regular versions which came laced with both sugar *and* artificial sweeteners. MAFF's response was not to insist that manufacturers cut the amount of saccharin in drinks, but to double the recommended maximum daily intake. This way they thought they could eliminate the 'problem'. But they failed to take account of the massive increase in the use of saccharin that followed de-regulation of the soft drinks industry, coupled with the low price of artificial sweeteners compared to sugar.

By 1993 the Government's own research was finding one in twelve (8 per cent) of two-year-olds exceeding the new 'safe' level of 5 mg/kg body weight/day. If the previous more cautious 'safe' level was used then it's estimated that one-third of two-year-olds would be exceeding the acceptable limit. MAFF finally asked manufacturers to do something – but only to advise extra dilution of saccharin-containing drinks for younger children. Ready-to-drink products were not included.

If that's not worrying enough – tests by Surrey County Council in 1996 found nearly one in twelve soft drinks, including leading brands and supermarket own-label drinks, contained levels of saccharin above the legal maximum.

To help parents check whether drinks contain artificial sweeteners, new rules mean that manufacturers must declare their presence next to the name of the product. But many coy manufacturers are circumventing the spirit of this law by putting it in small print on the back of labels.

Allergies and Hyperactivity

It is sometimes easy to believe that allergies are responsible for all kinds of childhood ills, yet parents can find it difficult to get the help and right advice they need – even in cases where there is a genuine, identified problem.

Food allergies are commonest in children during the first three years of life; 90 per cent grow out of their allergies by the age of five. Cows' milk, wheat and eggs are the most common trigger foods. Peanuts, other nuts and shellfish can also cause allergic reactions, though much less often. Soya, used to make formula milks for babies who are allergic to cows'-milk based formulas, can also cause allergies. Breastfeeding can reduce the risk, although in severe cases allergy-causing substances in the mother's own diet can pass through breastmilk to the baby. To minimise the risk of allergies it's advised that solids should not be started until after the age of four months, unmodified cows' milk should not be introduced until after one year and wheat and eggs should be delayed until at least six months and possibly later in families where there is a history of allergies.

Food allergy is a general catch-all term for all kinds of reactions to food and its ingredients, not all of which are correctly called 'allergies' in the medical sense. When there is a true food allergy the body's immune system reacts, launching an all-out attack and making antibodies to the allergen, which is what can cause a runny nose, itching eyes, breathing difficulties, diarrhoea and, in some cases, skin reactions. The same kind of reaction occurs in hayfever or asthma. Reaction to a food is immediate – the tongue and lips may swell and the person may even collapse or die unless there is speedy medical intervention. Fortunately few people suffer in this way, but those who do must of course take great care about what they eat. More and more youngsters suffer from peanut allergy. It's not clear why, but one theory links it to the use of peanut oil in baby formula milks or the mother's consumption of peanuts during pregnancy.

Other less severe reactions are more correctly termed intolerant reactions. In children symptoms include colic, runny nose, hyperactivity, asthma, eczema and urticaria. It is not clear how many people may be affected: some researchers put it at less than 1 per cent, others nearer 20–30 per cent. Other types of food intolerance may have a pharmacological cause, such as migraine brought on by chocolate, red wine or cheese.

Parents often worry that food additives may cause hyperactivity and other symptoms in children. However, the true incidence of intolerance to additives has been found to be lower than is often thought. A small number of children are sensitive to synthetic food colourings and some preservatives (as well as other foods) and may become hyperactive, though this needs to be properly diagnosed and should not be confused with other family problems or the normal boisterousness of small children.

If you think your child may have a problem of this kind it's important to seek medical advice. Although some sufferers do find an elimination diet (which helps to identify foods which may trigger reactions) to be helpful, this should never be attempted, particularly for children, without medical supervision.

PEANUT ALLERGY

Recent estimates have put the number of children allergic to peanuts at over 65,000 in the UK, with over a thousand at risk of anaphylactic shock and sudden death. Quite why an increasing number of children are sensitive to peanuts is not fully understood, but some experts believe the use of oils derived from peanuts in baby foods, milk and even nipple cream could be to blame. There's also a genetic factor – about a quarter of children have a genetic predisposition to developing allergies and if they are exposed to allergenic chemicals at an early age it can sensitise their immune system.

Now some manufacturers are reformulating products to exclude peanut derivatives, but it is not always easy to tell from labels if peanuts or their products might be in foods (*see 'Hidden Peanuts', page 10*).

Slim Hopes

Supermarkets shelves sag under the weight of 'low-fat', 'lite', 'diet', 'low-calorie' and 'sugar-free' products – yet the sad truth is that, as a nation, we are getting fatter. The latest statistics are the worst on record. About half the population is overweight and obesity has doubled in the last 10 years so that now nearly one in six people is obese – that is, so overweight that it's damaging their health. If current trends continue, nearly a quarter of women and a fifth of men will be obese by 2005.[1]

But if you turned to this chapter to find out what dieting products or programmes this book recommends to remedy these disastrous health statistics, you'll be sadly disappointed. The message of this chapter is simple: don't diet. The diet to help you stay in shape is the same diet as the one that will keep you healthy. In the long term diets don't work, some dieting products can be dangerous to health, dieting can make you obsessive and fearful of food, and the pounds you're most likely to lose are from your purse.

Each year as we chase our dreams we spend £1 billion feeding an ever-hungry diet industry. It's all too easy to believe that all we need to feel great and confident (and who doesn't want to feel great and confident?) is the latest diet programme, slimming club, meal-replacement food, diet book, video, exercise gimmick, pills, potions ... the list is almost endless. But with no effective laws to protect us from unscrupulous advertisers and with misleading products legally on sale, it's easy to get hooked onto the dieting treadmill.

Why Diets Don't Work

The dream that a physical ideal can be achieved through the latest diet fad retains its appeal despite the fact that the majority of people who embark upon diets to lose weight fail to do so in the long term. It's relatively easy to lose weight in the short term. The energy equation is a simple one: if you eat fewer calories than you burn up you'll lose weight. But the difficulty for many people is in maintaining the weight loss.

One of the main reasons diets don't work is because they undermine normal regulatory eating messages such as hunger and fullness, which can lead to overeating. Another reason is that cutting back on calories causes the body to lower its metabolic rate – so you actually burn up fewer calories – a survival mechanism from times when humans faced periods of famine.

Many long-term dieters will be familiar with yo-yo dieting. You go on a new diet, full of optimism and delighted when you start to lose some weight. But soon you become bored with the same old meal-replacement biscuits or mixes, or diet regime. Your determination starts to wane and you give in to temptation with a large piece of chocolate cake. Feeling guilty and depressed, you eat more chocolate cake. Feeling even more guilty you give up on the diet, the pounds pile back on and you feel a failure. Until you start the next new diet ...

Not only is yo-yo dieting bad for self-esteem, it's bad for health. Medical research[2] has now found that a cycle of fast weight loss followed by weight gain can lead to:

- decreases in lean tissue
- loss of bone minerals
- attacks of gout or gallstones
- sudden heart attacks
- hair loss
- fibrosis and scarring of tissue
- high blood pressure when returning to a normal diet
- depression
- shortened lifespan.

In addition, appetite-depressant drugs can have harmful side-effects.

Experts recommend that dieters should aim for safe and steady weight loss. This is no more than an average of 1–2 lb (0–5 to 1.0 kg) a week, achieved by cutting calories by 500–1,000 calories a day.[3]

Measuring Fatness

Body mass index (BMI) is the way in which fatness is usually measured. This is calculated by dividing body weight (in kilograms) by height squared (in metres). But you don't need a calculator – BMI charts are widely available which plot height on one axis and weight on the other, so at a glance you can easily discover your BMI. Weight is normally classified as follows:

	BMI
underweight	20 or less
'normal' weight	20–25
overweight	25 – 30
obese	over 30

While this can be a useful measure, it has a number of limitations. BMI does not distinguish between heaviness due to fat and that due to muscle. Nor does it distinguish the location of the fat – fat round the middle is more of a health risk (*see 'Apples and Pears',* *page 123*).

The No-diet Diet

The only diet this book recommends is the 'no-diet' diet.[4] Forget about restrictive, boring calorie counting and – instead of being afraid even to look at a decent-sized meal – start eating and enjoying your food. What's important is not the weight you are but the shape you are in.

So stop climbing onto the scales every morning and take a fresh look at what you're eating and your lifestyle. Do you eat a reasonably healthy diet – not too much fatty and processed foods and snacks? Are your meals based around starchy foods such as rice, pasta, potatoes and bread with plenty of fresh fruit and vegetables? Are you reasonably fit and active?

Amazingly, one of the easiest ways to lose weight is to write down everything you eat and drink for a few typical days (no cheating!). It's often surprising to discover just what you do eat, and when. Do you skip breakfast but then eat a chocolate bar, bag of crisps or jam doughnut mid-morning? Do you eat more when you are stressed, bored or in love? By understanding your own eating preferences and emotional responses to food you can start to make changes that will not only help you to eat more healthily but also to maintain a healthy weight.

If you genuinely are overweight for your size and age (too many dieters are people of normal weight), by following a healthy diet and lifestyle you'll find that you will shed some of the pounds. It won't happen overnight: there are no magic ways to lose weight fast (and for it to stay off) despite what the adverts say. And slow weight loss (1–2 lb a week) is far more likely to be permanent weight loss. Ask your GP to refer you to a state registered dietitian for advice; if you do join a slimming club make sure it's one that isn't obsessed with calorie counting and weekly weigh-ins, but instead offers support and dietary advice based on sensible, healthy eating.

Finally, this 'no-diet' diet does involve a certain amount of self-acceptance. The rise of the super-thin supermodels has given us a false sense of beauty and it's easy to forget that the rest of us come in all different shapes and sizes. If you want to feel more confident, don't go on a diet – join an assertiveness course. Stepping off the dieting treadmill can be a liberation. Not only does it mean an end to the tedium and guilt of calorie counting, it also means you can enjoy real, tasty, nutritious food and still feel and look great.

Why Are We Getting Fatter?

On the face of it, the answer is simple. It doesn't take a genius to know that it's a question of energy imbalance. If you eat more calories than you burn up, then an extra inch here and there is the inevitable result. But the whole picture is far more complicated.

Our increasingly sedentary lifestyles are at the root of the problem. Many people's jobs are less active than those of a generation or two ago, and labour-saving devices in the home mean modern housekeeping takes less time and energy than in our grandparents' day. The rise in obesity not only parallels growing car ownership but also the number of hours spent watching TV, which has doubled since the mid-1960s to 26 hours a week. Central heating also means we use up less energy. Watching television in a warm room uses up as little energy as sleeping.

Over the last couple of generations we've compensated for our more leisurely lifestyles by eating somewhat less, but not sufficiently less. What also has changed dramatically in the last 50 years is *what* we eat. Since the war we eat a lot less starchy carbohydrate foods but a lot more fat, mainly in processed foods. And as fat is twice as fattening, ounce for ounce, as other foods it's easy to see why we've piled on the pounds.

METABOLIC MYTHS

How many times have you heard people say *'I hardly eat a thing but the pounds still pile on. I must have a slow metabolism'?* Unfortunately this is a myth. Overweight people, in fact, use *more* calories, not fewer. Researchers at the Dunn Nutrition Unit in Cambridge have found that overweight people have a *higher* metabolic rate than people of normal weight, but that they regularly underestimate how much they eat.

EXERCISE ANSWERS

Taking exercise will help you to keep healthy and maintain a healthy weight but the pounds won't drop off quickly by exercise alone. Half an hour of aerobics will burn up only around 200 calories – that's about a chocolate bar's worth. But, over time, taking moderate regular exercise will improve health and well-being, help maintain steady weight loss and ensure that the pounds don't pile on again. And you don't have to take up jogging or join a gym. Brisk walking and incorporating more activity into your daily life, such as walking to the shops or walking up stairs instead of using the lift at work, will help to improve fitness.

Apples and Pears

Our weight tends to increase as we get older, but research suggests what is more important is the type of fat we carry around, rather than the amount. The good news is that those bulging thighs or bottom are not such a health threat as we may fear. In fact, it's the fat that we can't see – the fat around our internal organs – which is far more likely to be the cause of heart attacks. That's why those people who are apple-shaped – fatter around the middle – are at greater risk than the classic 'pear-shaped' person.

IT'S ALL IN THE GENES – OR IS IT?

There is some truth in the link between your genes and your pre-disposition to put on weight. But only for some people. According to Dr Andrew Prentice, head of obesity research at the Dunn Nutrition Unit in Cambridge, less than 25 per cent of obesity is due to genetic problems – our lifestyles and what we eat are far more important.

Yet scientists think they have identified a gene for obesity – at least in laboratory mice – which they can treat with a genetically-engineered hormone. It may work on mice, but not yet on humans – although with a quarter of UK women estimated to be obese by 2005, drug companies are working hard to discover a magic anti-fat remedy. So far such promises are no different from other 'miracle' diet claims – best taken with a pinch of salt (or even better, without one!).

STARTING YOUNG

Children may be getting taller for their age but they are also getting much fatter. Lack of exercise and poor diet are to blame, say researchers.

At the same time there is growing concern about the numbers of teenage and pre-adolescent young girls, some as young as seven, who are dieting although they are not overweight. Under-nutrition at a time of physical growth and development can lead to retarded growth, delayed puberty and to osteoporosis later in life, and dieting can affect mental and learning abilities.

Equally worrying, over-concern about food and weight can lead to eating problems and, in more severe cases, anorexia and bulimia. Anorexia is a complex and distressing condition which needs sympathetic and professional treatment (*see Appendix for a contact address for the Eating Disorders Association*). While dieting itself is unlikely to 'cause' anorexia, research has found that teenage girls who diet are eight times more likely to develop eating disorders than non-dieters.[5]

The Diet Food Industry

As slimming became a national obsession, diet food manufacturers were only too happy to cash in on people's anxieties about their weight with meal-replacement foods and very-low-calorie total diet plans. But as slimming has begun to fall out of favour and health has become the new buzz word, companies have started repositioning these same products as 'health' foods. At the same time, a whole host of low-fat, low-calorie foods, from spreads, sausages, cream and cakes to drinks and desserts, hold out the promise that we really can have our cake and eat it. But is the dream too good to be true?

VERY-LOW-CALORIE DIETS

These total diet plans, which supply all the food you need, have largely fallen out of favour following a critical Government report and adverse publicity. Some products offered as few as 400 calories a day. Not only were they difficult to stick to, but fast weight loss is dangerous to health. Now very-low-calorie diets offer around 800–1,000 calories a day, though even this is considered low by dietitians. If you can stick to such a restrictive regime you will lose weight, but such products tend to fail in the long run because they do nothing to re-educate eating habits and they perpetuate yo-yo dieting.

MEAL-REPLACEMENT SLIMMING FOODS

Meal replacements are typically sold either as biscuits or bars, or as mixes for drinks and other concoctions. They are generally designed to be eaten two to three times a day, with slimmers eating one 'calorie-controlled' meal of their choice as well during the day. Many such products are now sold not just as slimming aids but as 'health' foods, making claims such as 'a healthy aid to weight maintenance'. But there's little to justify their 'healthy' marketing image, according to a survey by the Food Commission which found that meal-replacement foods may be no healthier than a chocolate biscuit or milk shake.[6] The Food Commission gave most products the thumbs down for:

- **poor nutrition** – many products were high in fat and/or sugar, low in protein and fibre. New EC rules mean products will have to meet nutritional specifications on protein and fat, and to include essential vitamins and minerals;
- **not being lower in calories** – in general, products were not significantly lower in calories than many snack foods;
- **encouraging people to lose weight too quickly** – fast weight loss can be dangerous to health;
- **encouraging unhealthy eating habits** – because of their emphasis on sweet and often high-fat snack habits;

- **failing to change eating habits** – virtually all suggested continued use even once ideal weight was reached.
- **selling less for more** – for their content, meal-replacement products are expensive.

New European rules that toughen up on standards for meal-replacement foods mean that products will no longer be able to make any claims about the amount or speed of weight loss or their ability to satisfy hunger in their advertising or labelling.

LOW-CALORIE READY MEALS

Low-calorie ready meals offer convenience to would-be weight watchers, although criticism of small portions led to some products being dubbed 'mean cuisine'. As with meal-replacement foods, manufacturers have seen a bigger marketing opportunity by offering their meals as 'healthy' convenience foods. But a survey of 75 meals by the Coronary Prevention Group (CPG) said you'll need to choose carefully to ensure that such meals genuinely offer low-calorie, healthy eating.[7]

All meals examined were high in salt, many were low in fibre and carbohydrate and they were only slightly more likely to meet nutritional recommendations for fat than comparative 'regular' ready meals. The researchers also concluded that, as processed foods, they were likely to be lower in vitamins and nutrients than homemade foods. Although often sold as complete meals, the CPG advise serving such meals with fresh vegetables, salad and bread to achieve a healthier meal.

DIET FOODS AND DRINKS

Fuelled by a late-twentieth-century obsession that equates thinness with beauty and happiness, so-called 'diet' foods and drinks have taken the market by storm. There's been a phenomenal growth in the market for a host of soft drinks, table-top sweeteners and desserts sweetened not with sugar but with artificial sweeteners such as aspartame (NutraSweet), saccharin and acesulfame-K. These sweeteners provide the taste of sugar, or an approximation of it, but none of the calories. So popular is their use by manufacturers that they can now be found in all kinds of 'low-calorie' and well as many regular foods, including savoury ones.

But this success story hides two disturbing findings. First, the growth in the use of artificial sweeteners has not led to an overall decline in our sugar consumption. We might be adding less sugar ourselves to our drinks and cooking, but we're eating more hidden sugars in processed foods and particularly in soft drinks.

Secondly is the lack of any scientifically adequate evidence that the way many people substitute intense sweeteners for sugar helps in the reduction of weight or the prevention of obesity. Indeed, research indicates that the effect of a sweet taste on the palate, whether in the form of sugar or artificial sweeteners, is to stimulate the appetite, not suppress it. The mechanisms which control hunger and appetite are complex; the consumption of calories in one form or another plays a key role in the satiation of hunger. Food without these calories, as in the case of artificial sweeteners, is unlikely to suppress hunger.

And what's more, some artificial sweeteners may actually boost appetite. In tests, increasing the sweetness of foods – whether by sugar or artificial sweeteners – increased the appetites of human volunteers. But saccharin had a particularly pronounced effect – not only did volunteers make up for lost calories but they also ate significantly more throughout the day – on average a further 200 calories.

The growing conclusion is that intense sweeteners offer little or no help to would-be dieters unless they make substantial changes to their diet overall.

LOW-FAT/LOW-CALORIE FOODS

As slimming foods have fallen out of favour, we've swallowed the idea that foods with less fat and calories are the answer to our unhealthy, fattening diet. All we need do is eat more and weigh less – at least that's the dream that the admen try and sell us. But it's not working. There's growing evidence that this promise really is too good to be true. Surprisingly, using fat-reduced and other 'low-cal' foods are not such an effective way of cutting calories for many people. The reason is too many of us compensate for the 'lost calories' by eating more, either unwittingly or as a treat.

The problem with much low-calorie, low-fat food is that it is still highly processed, low-nutrient food, what many people would call junk food. So can replacing high-fat junk food with low-fat junk food really be the answer? It certainly doesn't look that way from the US, where low-cal and lite foods have been around a lot longer than here. Americans are even more obese than us Brits.

NO-FAT FOODS

Imagine: foods with all the yumminess of high-fat ones but with none of the fat (*see 'Fat Substitutes', page 130*). Such 'no-fat' foods sound like a ultimate dieter's dream where you can eat to your heart's content with no guilt or expanding waistline. But dream on ...

Olestra

It's been given approval in the US for use in savoury snacks and it could be here soon. Olestra (brand name Olean) is the invention of Procter & Gamble. It claims to provide all the taste and 'mouth-feel' (as it is known in the trade) of fat but with none of the calories. Its makers have cleverly altered its chemical structure so that our bodies can't digest it. Eat as much as you like and it won't provide any fat or calories.

But, like every promise that sounds too good to be true, there's a downside. Olestra is virtually unique among food additives and ingredients in that it can actually deprive the body of valuable nutrients. As it passes through the digestive system it soaks up fat-soluble nutrients including vitamins A, D, E and K,

carotenoids and sterols, which play a vital role in protecting against heart disease, various cancers, stroke and age-related irreversible blindness and cataracts. In addition it can cause a whole range of unpleasant side-effects, including stomach cramps, diarrhoea, what has been termed 'anal leakage' and the unpleasant sounding 'oil-in-toilet' after a bowel movement.[8]

In the US, Olestra has been given limited approval for use in savoury snacks, crisps and biscuits. Products containing Olestra will have to be fortified with vitamins and carry the warning: 'Olestra may cause abdominal cramping and loose stools. Olestra inhibits absorption of some vitamins and other nutrients. Vitamins A, D, E and K have been added.'

The decision about whether Olestra will be approved in the UK has yet to be taken. But many consumer and health organisations say Olestra would be an unwelcome and unnecessary food additive as it's unlikely to encourage better eating habits or help achieve sustained weight loss. In fact in the US it's been reported that products containing Olestra are seen as a green light by people to eat as much as they want. Products might be 'fat-free' but they are certainly not calorie-free.

Fat Substitutes

Here are just some of the fat substitutes that are already approved or in the pipeline:

- **Simplesse** – launched in 1992, this is made from milk protein and so avoids the tag of 'artificial additive'. It is not suitable for vegetarians.
  Calorific value: 1.33 kcal/g
  Uses: 5 per cent fat low-fat spread, yoghurts and desserts, soups, ice cream, processed cheese, dips, mayonnaise and spreads.
- **Olestra** – a sucrose polyester which passes through the body undigested. Under consideration for approval in the UK.

Calorific value: 0

Uses: Approved for use in savoury snacks and biscuits in the US. Can be used for frying.

- **Litesse** – a carbohydrate-based bulking agent which is approved by the EC.

Calorific value: 1 kcal/g

Uses: Ice cream, frozen desserts, cake, cookies and confectionery.

- **Salatrim** – a combination of fat and fat substitutes derived from vinegar, cheese and vegetable oils. Being considered for approval in the UK.

Calorific value: 5 kcal/g

Uses: Plans for use in low-fat chocolate bars, ice cream and cheese.

- **Paselli** – the Paselli range of fat substitutes is made from hydrolysed potato starch.

Calorific value: 1–3.8 kcal/g depending on the type.

Uses: Reduced-fat mayonnaise and salad dressings, low-fat ice creams and frozen desserts, cheesecakes and pates, cooked meat products.

- **Slendid** – a fibre-based fat substitute which is made from the pectin found in the peel of citrus fruits. It was launched in 1991.

Calorific value: 0

Uses: Salad dressings, mayonnaise, soups, sauces, frozen desserts and toppings, processed cheeses, yoghurts and baked goods such as cheesecake.

Source: Leatherhead Food Research Association

NB With the exception of Olestra, which is classified as an additive and must be declared on labels, you are unlikely to find fat substitutes declared by their names on the label. Most manufacturers choose to label their more 'natural' sounding ingredients. Most products containing Simplesse, for example, will only declare 'milk protein' in the ingredients list.

FAT BUSTERS

Don't believe the claims of products claiming to be 'fat busters', 'fat burners' or 'fat absorbers'. There's no evidence that these products work – and even if they did they could be dangerous. One product, criticised for making untrue claims by the Advertising Standards Authority, claimed to work because the ingredient Chitosan had been used to clean up polluted water!

APPETITE SUPPRESSANTS AND SLIMMING PILLS

There has been much concern about the easy availability of these kinds of drugs over the counter, or through slimming clinics, often at great expense and with inadequate health checks. Such drugs can have serious side-effects, some can be addictive, and their use should be a last resort for those with serious weight problems under strict medical supervision and for limited periods.

MIRACLE SLIMMING PRODUCTS/DIET FADS

The kinds of products and diet regimes that fall into this category are too numerous to mention. Whatever the claims, don't be tempted to part with your money. Lax laws mean rogue companies are getting away with over-the-top and untrue claims.

Advertisers' Dream

Many people believe that claims for miracle diet aids must be true or else they wouldn't be allowed to advertise. But this (understandable) belief is, unfortunately, wrong. The Advertising Standards Authority is responsible for policing adverts, yet its own surveys have found that many slimming advertisements fall foul of its rules. In 1996 the National Food Alliance called for pre-vetting of slimming ads and for more effective sanctions against transgressors, after its survey of adverts for slimming products and services – including creams, pills, slimming clubs, body wraps, books and

---

videos, slimming foods and supplements in women's magazines and popular newspapers – found that the majority did not comply with the ASA's rules. And many were making claims that were misleading or untrue.[9]

Advertising plays an important role in maintaining the myth of 'miracle' or easy weight loss. Slimming adverts are a special area: because of the vulnerability and often desperation of those who have sought (usually unsuccessfully) to lose weight permanently, many of those reading these adverts are likely to want to believe the claims (however outrageous) that are made. Although it's tempting to believe such claims – don't. Products that offer a quick-fix solution to weight problems are a con. If you see an advert or other promotional literature that you think sounds too good to be true, complain to the ASA or contact your local trading standards department (*see Appendix: Taking Action*).

Label Confusion

Despite the name 'diet', drinks and foods don't contain any magic ingredient that will help us shed unwanted pounds. So, are claims of 'diet' on the label misleading by implying special properties for weight reduction? By law any label or advertisement for a slimming product must add the proviso that it be used as 'part of a calorie-controlled diet'. But this is pretty meaningless. Any food, even a chocolate bar, if eaten 'as part of a calorie-controlled diet' could make this claim. It would be far better for all slimming and diet products to include the words: 'This food cannot help slimming or weight control in itself. This can only be achieved by eating a calorie controlled diet.'

However, to most people a 'diet' claim will lead them to believe that the product has advantages for weight loss. The danger for dieters is that if they believe 'diet' products will automatically help them control their calorie intakes, then they are more likely to believe they can eat more. Using no-cal sweeteners and then treating yourself to a creamcake (as one advertisement for a sweetener implied you could do) will be counterproductive.

This is not the only way shoppers with an eye on their waistline can have the wool pulled over their eyes.

Slimming Tricks of the Trade

You'd normally expect foods sold as 'slimming' to be made with fewer calories, less fat or less sugar – but don't count on it. Watch out for the following slimming tricks of the trade:

- crisps sold for slimmers by one retailer actually had, weight for weight, more calories, more fat and three times the salt of the company's low-fat crisps. The only difference was that the 'slimming' crisps came in a small bag.
- slimming or low-calorie chocolate may not be significantly lower in calories than regular chocolate confectionery – one brand actually had more calories, weight for weight, than a Cadbury's *Fruit and Nut* bar. The difference was that the slimming ones come in smaller bars.
- similarly, shoppers buying 'cup-a-soup' for slimmers might think they were buying a special formulation. But again they'd be wrong. A leading brand manufacturer's 'slimmer' and 'regular' cup-a-soups were virtually the same – except that the 'slimmers' version contained only about half the quantity of the regular version, and at a premium price, too.
- some bread may come labelled as 'light' or 'lite'. But don't necessarily expect significantly fewer calories weight for weight. Light may just refer to the texture, not the calories.
- chocolate chip cookies aimed at slimmers had virtually the same number of calories per biscuit as regular cookies but a price that was over 50 per cent more.
- a cereal aimed at slimmers boasted 'low-calorie, high-fibre' credentials but actually had more calories and half the fibre of *All Bran* and no more fibre than cereals without added bran such as *Shredded Wheat* and *Weetaflakes*.

- 'light' digestive biscuits boasting 25 per cent less fat sound good for slimmers. But the small print shows that the calories per biscuit have only dropped from 73 to 69 – a cut of barely 5 per cent.

Eat Your Greens

There are many good reasons to eat plenty of vegetables and fruit. They are not only naturally delicious but also packed full of vital vitamins, minerals and other substances which keep us healthy. We were always told to eat our greens, but now we know why – it won't make your hair curl – but it will help protect you from a whole range of diseases including the major killers heart disease and cancer. They also provide fibre and are low in fat and calories, so choosing them instead of fatty, sugary foods can help keep you a healthy weight.

One of the most exciting nutritional developments in recent years has been the discovery that some of the vitamins and other substances that vegetables and fruit contain are antioxidants, having a protective role against heart disease, cataracts, certain cancers and perhaps much more – they may even help us to live longer. So far scientists think there are over 40,000 such phyto-chemicals – literally plant chemicals – in fruit and veg, but they are only just beginning to understand how they work.

This is the cutting edge of nutritional science and there is un-doubtedly more to be discovered, but we can be sure that fruit and vegetables are good for us in a variety of ways, and that the more of them you eat, the better – preferably at least five portions a day.

What Are Antioxidants?

A number of vitamins and other phytochemicals are now known to be antioxidants. As their name suggests, antioxidants protect against the degenerative process of oxidation in the cells of our body, helping to prevent disease. Antioxidants include vitamins C and E and carotenes (which the body converts into vitamin A), and the mineral selenium. Many other phytochemicals help to maintain our health.

Antioxidants work by neutralising damaging 'free radicals', which are the by-product of normal cell activity but which can also be created by chemical pollutants and cigarette smoke. It is the damage to cells caused by free radicals that is believed to be the start of diseases such as heart disease and cancer. While there is still more work to be done, the lower levels of fruit and vegetables eaten in Britain compared with many other European countries may explain our higher rates of heart disease and some cancers.

PHYTOCHEMICALS AT WORK

- **Carotenoids** – there are more than 500 carotenoids, found in green leafy vegetables, yellow/orange vegetables and fruits. Carotenoids are converted to vitamin A in our body. Carotenoids include **Lutein** and **Lycopenes**, found in large quantities in tomatoes. Good sources of carotenoids include sweet potatoes, carrots, spinach, pumpkin, red peppers, mango, apricots, cabbage, broccoli and tomatoes.
- **Vitamin C** – found almost exclusively in fruit and vegetables, vitamin C is destroyed by cooking, so eat as much raw fruit and veg as possible or cook lightly such as steaming, microwaving or stir-frying rather than boiling. Good sources include red and green

peppers, strawberries, blackcurrants, oranges, grapefruit, kiwi fruit, banana, cabbage, potatoes, peas and pineapple.

- **Vitamin E** – found in vegetable oils, nuts and seeds, with modest amounts in most fruit and vegetables especially avocados, mango, blackberries, spinach and broccoli.

- **Selenium** – good sources are cereals, especially wholegrain bread, fish, liver, pork, cheese, eggs, hazelnuts, brazil nuts. Modern agriculture has stripped the soil of much of this mineral.

- **Flavonoids** – found in tea, especially green tea, onions and wine.

- **Limonene** – found in citrus fruit oils.

- **Folic Acid** – a B vitamin found in dark green leafy vegetables and cereals. May protect cells in pre-cancerous condition.

- **Isothiocyanates and Indoles** – found in broccoli, Brussels sprouts, cabbage, cauliflower, turnips, kale and kohlrabi – have anti-cancer properties.

- **Allicin** – found in garlic and onions. Has anti-bacterial properties and may stimulate the production of detoxifying enzymes.

At Least Five a Day

We Brits eat less fruit and veg than virtually every other country in Europe, which goes a long way towards explaining why we have such high rates of diet-related disease such as heart disease and cancer. On average we manage only a measly three portions of fruit and veg a day – compared to the nine that the Greeks enjoy. And while some people undoubtedly eat more than the average, that leaves many eating even less – particularly people in Scotland and the North, those on low incomes and, sadly, many young people. Two-thirds of today's 16–24 year olds eat fruit less than once a week.

Now health campaigners want to see a national 'at least 5 a day' campaign like the successful drives in the US and Australia.

Pill Poppers

The question many people ask is whether the same benefits of eating fruit and veg can be gained from a daily dose of pills. Whether you find broccoli a bore or turnips a turnoff, or whether you just want the added insurance that you are getting your daily allowance, there's a vast choice of supplements to choose from. But on current evidence the answer is no – whatever their ingredients, supplements just can't match the real thing. Although there's excellent evidence that eating more vegetables and fruit has real health benefits, as yet no one fully understands which of the myriad vitamins, minerals and other micronutrients found in fruit and veg are the key health promoters. Vitamin pill companies now offer more and more exotic combinations, but new evidence warns that supplements are unlikely to match the effects of eating fruit and veg, and may even be harmful.[1] One study found that men who took beta-carotene supplements were *more likely* to develop heart disease and lung cancer. Beta-carotene is just one of several hundred different carotenoids, and taking large doses of just one may upset the body's natural functioning.

Beware of claims made for dietary supplements. A daily multivitamin pill is unlikely to do you any harm but it's unlikely to match the full health benefits of eating fruit and veg. It's much better, often cheaper and certainly tastier to stick to the fresh fruit and veg.

Super-veg

We are now being promised 'super-veg' – the chance to get added health benefits along with our broccoli and tomatoes. Scientists are tweaking the genes of ordinary veg to create super-veg with more health-enhancing chemicals. So far scientists are breeding broccoli with higher levels of the isothiocyanate phytochemical, sulphoraphane. This is the substance that gives Brussels sprouts their characteristic flavour and which it is thought can destroy cancer cells. At the same time, tomatoes are being tweaked to add extra lycopene.

The promise is that we will be able to get our five portions of fruit and veg a day by only eating two or three. It's still at the research stage and too early to tell whether the genetic changes will have any undesirable effects such as producing unpleasant-tasting broccoli. And of course there is no knowing whether consumers will take to the idea of beefed-up broccoli or topped-up tomatoes.

Fresh v frozen

We're advised to eat at least five portions of fruit and veg a day. Fresh raw fruit and veg has the most vitamins, but if you're cooking veg, which is better nutritionally – fresh or frozen? The answer may surprise you. Fresh vegetables generally contain the highest levels of vitamins, as processing can destroy vitamins such as vitamin C. But some frozen veg may actually contain more vitamin C than fresh. That's because many frozen veg are quick-frozen very soon after harvesting, while 'fresh' vegetables may be several days or sometimes weeks old by the time you buy them, and gradually lose their vitamins with time. So avoid limp, wilted or shrivelled veg and be careful how you cook them. Whether fresh or frozen, prolonged boiling will destroy vitamins – steaming, microwaving or stir-frying are the healthiest ways to cook vegetables.

Canned fruit and vegetables generally contain lower levels of vitamins but are still a useful source – especially if you choose low-sugar or low-salt varieties.

Pesticides

When you're piling the fruit and veg into your shopping trolley do you worry that you're getting a hidden dose of unwanted chemicals along with all that goodness? The trouble is there's no way to tell. There's nothing on the label to inform us which added extras we might be getting. We can't see them and sometimes we can't even wash them off.

We've had scares about organophosphate chemicals in carrots and lindane in milk, even theories that mad cow disease could have been caused by pesticides. Surveys show that we are worried about pesticides, but are we right to be worried?

Unfortunately there's no simple answer. We're told that all pesticides used are rigorously tested, perfectly safe and legally licensed. The Government says that while small amounts of pesticide residues may sometimes be found there is no need for alarm because they are harmless and Government testing ensures that they are kept within safe levels. The good news is that, according to Government tests, not all fruit and veg contains residues. That's some reassurance, though testing is not always complete (*see 'Limits of Testing, page 145*). But what about those in which residues have been found? Results of Government tests published in 1996 found 44 per cent of fruit and vegetables sampled contained pesticide residues, with 2 per cent over the permitted Maximum Residue Level (MRL). So what are they doing there?

Residues can remain as a result of legal use of pesticides, either before or after harvest, or sometimes it can be the result of illegal use. Government tests do show that farmers sometimes overuse chemicals, that they sometimes use banned chemicals and that sometimes chemicals are found at higher than permitted levels in our food. That's far less reassuring and one of the main reasons why increasing numbers of people are now looking for food that is grown without the use of chemicals (*see 'Choosing Organic', page 158*).

Not So Reassuring

In 1997 parents were advised to peel fruit for children after 'higher than desirable' amounts of pesticide residues were found in a small number of apples and peaches. This latest revelation is the result of Government tests for organophosphate and carbamate insecticides on apples, pears, nectarines, peaches, oranges, tomatoes and carrots, which have found a tremendous variation in the amount of residues fruit and vegetables may contain – even between vegetables grown in the same field and treated in the same way. Scientists don't yet know why this happens; it's not the result of illegal or inappropriate spraying; but it does mean that small numbers of fruits and vegetables may routinely exceed safety levels. If unlucky enough to eat two such pieces of fruit, toddlers, the most at-risk group, may suffer an upset stomach, say Government scientists. This research throws into question residue testing results, which provide only average figures, and increases calls for a reduction in the use of and reliance on all pesticides in agriculture.

WHAT ARE PESTICIDES?

Modern farming has become more and more reliant on the intensive use of chemical pesticides and fertilisers. Pesticides are chemicals which are used to kill or control pests. Insecticides are used to kill insects, herbicides kill weeds, fungicides control fungus and moulds. Other chemicals are also used to control pests in the soil (soil sterilants), regulate plant growth (growth regulators) or to repel bird and animal pests. Fungicides and insecticides may also be used after harvest in crop storage, or during transport to prevent deterioration.

They've been part of the revolution in agriculture which has seen farming become highly mechanised and chemicalised. They've helped ensure crops are no longer devastated by pests, but at what cost? Pesticides are designed to be toxic but the problem is that they can also be poisonous to wildlife and other beneficial insects, and to human beings.

Ill-effects are hard to prove except in rare cases of poisoning when pesticides are misused. The World Health Organization (WHO) estimates that worldwide there are over three million cases of severe unintentional pesticide poisonings each year leading to 20,000 deaths, mostly in developing countries, though these figures may be an underestimate.

In the UK ordinary members of the public have become ill after being accidentally sprayed in their gardens or while out walking in the countryside, and farmers have suffered ill-health from the chemicals used in sheep-dips. But even in these cases it has been hard for sufferers to prove that pesticides were to blame.

It is rare for pesticide residues on food to cause poisoning, though it has happened. In 1985 in one of the worst cases, several hundred people in the US suffered severe stomach pains after eating watermelons contaminated with the pesticide aldicarb. The chemical had probably got into the water used to grow the fruit. In 1992 in Ireland at least 29 people were made ill by eating cucumbers that had been overtreated with aldicarb. And in 1995 the Ministry of Agriculture, Fisheries and Food (MAFF) warned that some carrots could cause stomach pains from the organophosphate insecticide used to treat carrot fly.

Such cases are thankfully rare, but the major concern with pesticide residues is the effects that a lifetime's exposure to minute amounts of pesticide residues in our food and drinking water may have. And nobody really knows what those effects may be. But there are fears that higher-than-average rates of breast cancer in areas of intensive farming may be linked to pesticide use, while other researchers believe that some people are sensitive to even minute amounts of pesticide residues and can suffer reactions such as migraine, abdominal pain, asthma and eczema, though this can be hard to prove. Falling sperm counts have also been blamed on pesticide residues.

Pesticides and Health

The increasing use of pesticides has led to widespread concern about their potential ill-effects on human health. The World Health Organization has said: *'The situation is particularly worrying in view of the lack of reliable data on the long-term consequences of exposure to pesticides.'*

While nearly 40 per cent of the 400 or so chemicals used as pesticides are known to be linked to cancer, reproduction hazards from impotency to birth defects, and genetic mutations or irritant reactions in laboratory tests on animals,[2] no causal link has been proven between pesticides and forms of cancer, nervous and allergic diseases and reproduction problems in humans.

However, the prestigious British Medical Association warns in its 1990 report, 'Pesticides, Chemicals and Health': *'There are serious doubts about the scientific validity of some of the studies that have been undertaken and there is no epidemiological evidence available for many pesticides. In other words we do not know whether many pesticides are harmful or not in day to day use.'* This lack of data and the inconclusive results of many studies should not lead to an assumption of safety, the report continues: *'The lack of observed harmful effects from a particular pesticide does not mean that it is therefore safe.'*

The report concludes: *'Until we have a more complete understanding of pesticide toxicity, the benefit of the doubt should be awarded to protecting the environment, the worker and the consumer. More particularly, where there are serious concerns relating to the safety of a particular pesticide, its use should be withdrawn or restricted until a new risk/benefit analysis can be made.'*

HOW ARE PESTICIDES CONTROLLED?

The Government regulates pesticides by approving them for safety and restricting how farmers can use them. However, many older, less safe chemicals are still in use because of delays in reassessing their safety. Since 1988 there have also been legal limits on the amount of residues which are allowed to remain in food – though this does not cover all pesticides which leave residues. These are known as MRLs – Maximum Residue Levels. In theory anyone who sells food with pesticides above the MRL can be prosecuted. Although MAFF's own testing finds about 1 per cent of food samples above the MRL, prosecutions rarely happen, sometimes because it is impossible to trace products back to the grower.

> **MRL**
> Maximum Residue Level – the highest level of residues which by law can remain in food. Not all pesticides have MRLs. They are not considered to be 'safety limits', more a way of checking whether pesticides have been used correctly.
>
> **ADI**
> Acceptable Daily Intake – the amount of a chemical which can be consumed every day for an individual's entire lifetime without any harm.

Limits of Testing

We're told we should be reassured by Government tests; what we are not told is the limits of such testing.

- tests are only carried out on a relatively small number of samples.
- not all pesticides are identified in tests. In the past, analyses have been found not to be sensitive enough to detect some residues, only about one-third of pesticides in use are actually tested for, while other residues become 'bound', particularly in cereals, and cannot be detected although they remain biologically active.
- figures provided are normally 'average' results which may mask significant variations.
- tests won't normally pick up other chemicals that may remain on food when pesticides break down or are concentrated during cooking or processing.
- some laboratory testing may not be accurate.
- the results of regular testing for pesticide residues by supermarkets, which would give consumers more information, are kept secret.

How Reliable Are Pesticide Tests?

To test the reliability of commercial laboratories, foods deliberately spiked with pesticides were sent by MAFF in 1992 to over 50 labs often used for Government testing. In one test bread was spiked with three pesticides, but only 44 out of 58 labs identified all three pesticides, while seven labs identified pesticides that weren't present. In a second test, only 18 of the labs correctly identified four pesticides in spiked beef fat. Even though the levels in bread were near to the maximum permitted (2,000 ug/kg), only two labs reported levels above 1,000 ug/kg, while the majority gave levels below 350 ug/kg. But the Government refused to name which laboratories had scored better than others.

Organophosphate Chemicals

Organophosphate (OP) pesticides are some of the most commonly used toxic pesticides, mainly used to kill insects. They were first developed from deadly nerve gases in Germany during the Second World War. But they can be sprayed quite legally on our food.

It's known that severe exposure to organophosphates can cause nausea, vomiting, stomach cramps and diarrhoea. In the worst cases this can lead to convulsions, coma and death. For years farmers have been battling to convince Government scientists that organophosphates used in sheep-dips have caused debilitating health effects such as impaired mental ability and chronic nerve damage.

And it was only in 1996, after much cover-up and confusion, that Government ministers admitted that exposure to organophosphates and other chemicals in the Gulf War was likely to be a possible cause of Gulf War Syndrome. In addition, an organic farmer, Mark Purdey, believes that BSE may have been caused or aggravated by the Government's insistence that cattle be sprayed with organophosphate pesticides.

So it is hard to feel reassured when traces of organophosphates turn up in carrots and apples.

WHERE ARE THE RESIDUES?

Pesticide residues can turn up in a wide variety of foods, including:

Carrots

We're advised to peel, top and tail our carrots – that's official advice. The same goes for parsnips. Three-quarters of carrots contain residues, with organophosphate chemicals causing particular problems. In 1995 MAFF issued warnings after unexpectedly high levels of organophosphate pesticides were found in carrots. Levels of up to 25 times higher than expected were found in 1–2 per cent of carrots, in some cases exceeding the Acceptable Daily Intake (ADI) level. Government advisors said the residues 'did not represent an immediate threat to health' but considered that levels should be kept below those considered safe. But the Government warned that consumers could experience an upset stomach from eating carrots with high levels of the chemical and should peel and remove the top of carrots – even though they admitted that some residues would nevertheless remain.

It transpired that farmers sometimes spray carrots up to nine times a year with organophosphates to control the carrot fly pest. MAFF recommended this should be reduced to a maximum of three sprayings, but new tests have showed only a slight decline in residues. Higher levels of organophosphates were found in UK carrots compared to imported carrots. No one knows why some carrots contain higher levels than others, but in the meantime organic carrot growers have benefited.

Apples

In 1997 parents were advised to peel fruit for children after 'higher than desirable' amounts of insecticide residues were found in a small number of apples and peaches.

Celery

Virtually all samples of celery tested have been found to contain pesticide residues, with over half containing more than one pesticide. Forty-one per cent of imported celery exceeded the maximum residues level (MRL) laid down by European law.

Milk

In 1996 the pesticide lindane, which is banned in several countries, was detected in nearly half of the UK milk supply. Nearly one pint in every 24 contains levels above the Maximum Residue Limit – the level triggering an investigation. Lindane doesn't break down easily and accumulates in the body. Chronic health effects associated with lindane exposure include birth and reproductive problems. The official line is that it's all perfectly safe. A Government minister assured consumers that the residue levels were low enough for the products 'to be eaten safely by consumers for their entire lives'. However, levels have increased – in 1989 only 15 per cent of milk samples contained the chemical.

What's worrying is it is not clear how this chemical is getting into milk. In the UK lindane is used to kill soil pests that attack rapeseed, wheat, turnips, swedes, sugar beet and winter barley. But not everyone thinks it's so safe. It is banned in 14 countries, including Sweden and the Netherlands, and severely restricted in many others. It's one of the so-called 'Dirty Dozen' pesticides that are considered to be particularly harmful by the international Pesticides Action Network. Yet in the UK it's still permitted, and in areas of intensive farming such as Lincolnshire there are fears that its use could be linked to clusters of breast cancer. Traces of the notorious chemical DDT, banned in the UK for over 10 years, have also been found in milk, though in less than 1 per cent of samples.

Potatoes

Nearly half the potatoes sampled in 1995 contained residues of aldicarb – a highly toxic insecticide suspected of being able to cause cancer.

Lettuce

Some commercial lettuce growers have been found to be spraying lettuce illegally with banned fungicides – banned because of the danger they pose to the workers spraying the chemical (it could make them sterile). Other lettuce has been found to contain residues of permitted chemicals but at levels above the allowed dose. Despite previous warnings some growers were found to be continually misusing pesticides.

Pears
One-third of British pears have been found to contain three pesticides not permitted for pears, including chlormequat, a growth regulator that is approved for cereals but not pears.

Chocolate
Chocolate bars from leading manufacturers have been found to contain traces of the highly toxic pesticide lindane.

Farmed Salmon
Eighty-one per cent of samples contained residues of the banned chemicals DDT or dieldrin, in results published in 1992.

Unless you buy organic produce you cannot be sure what added extras you may be getting.

Can Pesticides Be Washed Off?

Fruit and vegetables should always be washed thoroughly before eating, but don't assume that this will get rid of the pesticide residues. Some of the pesticides which are sprayed onto the surface of produce are likely to be removed, but some may have penetrated the skin. Other pesticides are known as 'systemic' – the chemical is taken up within the plant, so any traces cannot be washed off or removed by peeling. And while peeling helps to remove surface residues, you'll also be discarding good nutrients and fibre.

Strawberries and Suncream

Summer and strawberries go together like...strawberries and cream. Yet next summer perhaps it's the suncream you should be thinking about. Yes, those delicious summer fruits are helping to destroy the ozone layer.

The problem is the pesticide methyl bromide, which is commonly used to fumigate the soil before strawberries (as well as other salad crops) are grown. It's a potent pest killer and, while it doesn't leave residues on the fruit, it adds to the destruction of the ozone layer and thereby increases our risk of skin cancers and other health and environmental problems. In fact open-field strawberries, including pick-your-own, are the main users of the chemical – accounting for 75 per cent of all methyl bromide used for outdoor soil crops in the UK. It's also used in the production of some tomatoes, lettuce, cucumber, celery and mushrooms.

Industrialised countries have agreed to phase methyl bromide out by the year 2010. But as ozone depletion has now reached record levels and there are safe and effective alternatives for most uses, there are new calls for a more rapid phase-out. All strawberries grown in Germany and Denmark are already produced without methyl bromide, but it's still commonly used in the UK and in other countries such as Spain and the US, from which we import strawberries.

Environmental campaigners want supermarkets to sell and label produce that has been produced without the use of methyl bromide so that consumers are able to make environmentally-friendly choices.

P IS FOR PESTICIDES

Some foods such as fruit, cereals and vegetables are treated with pesticides after they have been harvested. Treated fruit, for example, will last longer and be less susceptible to damage in transport, while vegetables like potatoes can be sprayed to prevent sprouting. Somewhat worryingly, although tests are normally done for residues on skin and peel, Government advisors have discovered that the sprays can penetrate into the flesh of fruit, so consumers may be exposed to even higher dosages of these chemicals.

At one time there were plans from Brussels that foods treated with pesticides after harvest would have to be labelled. Some campaigners even proposed a 'P' numbering system like the E numbers used for food additives. But giving shoppers the right to know about the chemicals sprayed on their food was not popular with farmers or supermarkets and never got further than the drawing board.

HOW SAFE IS SAFE?

We're often told that the small amounts of pesticides which remain in some foods are safe. You may hear it being said that you'd need to eat impossibly huge quantities every day to be at risk. At the height of the scare about Alar 10 years ago we were told we'd need to eat 6,000 apples sprayed with Alar *a day* before we'd suffer any harm.

But this kind of argument, usually put out by the agrochemical industry, is a dishonest one. Chemicals, like pesticides, are tested for cancer by feeding them in large quantities to laboratory animals such as mice and rats. But that doesn't mean that much smaller levels over a long period of time may not also cause cancer. It may only happen in a very small number of cases, but it could still happen. In addition, chemicals are tested individually so nobody really has any idea what effects a cocktail of chemicals may have.

Any risks may be small, yet there can be no absolute guarantee of safety. It's a risk that many find acceptable. After all, pesticide residues are probably very small beer in the scale of life-threatening risks. We're told that we are much more likely to be knocked down by a bus. But there is a difference. If we are careful we can see the bus coming towards us. With pesticide residues there's nothing to see; we've no clear idea what kind of risk we are accepting.

This leaves us having to weigh up the risks for ourselves. It would be a big mistake to avoid fruit and vegetables because of fears about pesticide residues – the health benefits far outweigh any small risks. None the less, many people feel unhappy about having to accept this compromise and want to know why we can't have more food grown with fewer chemicals, or grown organically without their use at all.

CHILDREN AND PESTICIDES

Children are more likely to be at risk from pesticide residues than adults. That's because they eat more food relative to their weight than adults, and have a greater vulnerability to toxic chemicals. In infancy the kidneys and liver may not deal with pesticide residues as effectively; cancer-causing chemicals, for example, may have greater effect during periods of rapid cell division during infancy and early childhood. What's more, children have a whole lifetime ahead of them and thus more time for cancer to develop.

As a result of these differences, the US Academy of Sciences has recommended that, for children, permitted pesticide residues should be only 10 per cent of those allowed for adults. In the UK no special consideration is taken of children's possible greater risk despite a British Medical Association report which identified infants as a section of the population which might possibly be at risk from residues.

Kids at Risk

In 1989 the US Natural Resources Defense Council revealed that at least 17 per cent of the pre-school population – three million children – were exposed to toxic organophosphate insecticides from fruit and vegetables at levels above those which the US government considered safe.

Out of Sight, Out of Mind

When we go shopping, most of us think little about the conditions of agricultural workers in developing counties who produce much of our food. While we enjoy the pleasures of chocolate, women who work as pesticide sprayers on cocoa plantations in Malaysia commonly suffer skin irritations, rashes, headaches, tiredness or dizziness – the initial symptoms of pesticide poisoning. Many also suffer breathing difficulties, stomach pains and menstrual irregularities.

And it's not just cocoa. Whether it's bananas from Costa Rica, rice in India or many other cash crops in developing countries, pesticide poisonings are commonplace. In Costa Rica, around 100 people die and 10,000 are severely poisoned every year by the 55 million dollars' worth of pesticides drenched over Costa Rican vegetables and fruit destined for export. And in Kenya, workers on pineapple estates spray pesticides banned in developed countries. While minor food scares make front page news, this human misery, largely in developing countries, goes largely unreported.

Buying fairly-traded produce ensures that workers not only receive a fair wage for their labours but that working conditions are safe (*see 'Fairtrade', page 32*). Fairtrade campaigners want to see supermarkets, with their huge buying power, use their muscle to ensure that the food they sell has been produced safely and traded fairly.

Fertilisers

Traditional methods of keeping soil healthy and fertile, such as the addition of farm manure and crop rotation, have largely been replaced in intensive agriculture by the addition of chemical fertilisers. But now there are questions over the safety of some fertiliser residues in our food and drinking water.

Nitrates used in fertilisers to boost plant growth can end up in the vegetables themselves. In particular, some UK-grown lettuce and spinach have been found to contain high levels of nitrate residues. There's some evidence of a link between nitrates and stomach cancer, though it's not proven. Nitrates can in rare cases be a cause of blue-baby syndrome. The European Commission has decided that, in the interests of public health, there should be maximum levels on the amount of nitrates permitted in vegetables. However, MAFF is claiming a British 'victory'. It has won the right for UK spinach and lettuce to be allowed to contain higher levels of nitrates than permitted elsewhere in Europe. This might help UK growers but it's hardly in the interests of British consumers. Imported lettuce and spinach will have to comply with the European standards.

What's in Our Water?

With well-publicised scares over the safety of drinking water, sales of bottled water and water filters have boomed. By law drinking water should meet standards laid down by the EC for pesticides, nitrates, bacteria and metals such as aluminium and lead. But not all water manages to meet these high standards.

Recent results show that 99.5 per cent of tests on water, including those for pesticides, show it to be within safe levels. But that still leaves 21,000 drinking water samples containing pesticides above the legally acceptable limit of 0.1 µg/l.[3] And even this may be the tip of an iceberg – many common pesticides are not looked for, while others are not tested because it's too expensive. Friends of the Earth estimate that in 1992 over 14 million consumers in England at some time received drinking water containing pesticides above the legal standard.

Bacterial contamination from cryptosporidium and salmonella have also been a problem in some areas, while in others nitrates from farm fertilisers are contaminating ground water supplies in areas of intensive agriculture. Levels in drinking water have largely been brought within safe limits, however; we get more nitrates in our diet from vegetables than from drinking water.

Some households, particularly in Scotland, also receive water with too much lead. The main problem is from old lead piping. Lead is particularly dangerous for babies and young children as it can affect their intellectual development. The maximum permitted in UK drinking water is 50 μg/l – that's five times higher than the level which the World Health Organization thinks is safe. 'Safe' UK levels will fall in line with the WHO's, but not until well into the next century – 2010 at the earliest.

However, if you think the answer is to turn to bottled water you may be surprised that in comparison with drinking water most bottled waters are barely regulated and some don't justify their healthy image (*see 'What's In a Name? – Bottled Water', page 15*). Levels of bacteria in bottled water can be higher than those permitted in tap water, especially if it is kept once opened. If you use bottled water for babies, check that it is low in sodium and boil it first, as you would tap water.

THE HIDDEN COSTS OF INTENSIVE AGRICULTURE

World-wide intensive agriculture, with its reliance on chemical inputs, has helped to increase the amount of food grown and kept the price of our food down. We're told that cutting out chemicals would make food more expensive and put much of the world at risk of starvation. But what this argument ignores are the hidden costs of intensive agriculture which we all pay for in other ways. Take our drinking water, for example. Water bills have increased dramatically in recent years and we're told we have to pay more for cleaner water. Who would argue with cleaner water? But it's a shock to discover that it's costing us £121 million every year in Britain to monitor and remove pesticides from contaminated water supplies.

Intensive chemical farming has other detrimental effects on the environment. Larger field sizes to make farming more 'efficient' means fewer hedgerows, which in turn means fewer habitats for wildlife. Draining wetlands and 'improving' pastures have added to the loss. Intensive chemical farming, which destroys habitats and food supplies for wildlife, means Britain's most common birds, including the skylark, swallow and grey partridge, are in decline. Greater numbers of birds such as the skylark have been found on organic farms compared with conventional farmland. The Royal Society for the Protection of Birds (RSPB) is calling for a tax on pesticides to help save birds.

Pollution of rivers and soil erosion are also major problems. Plus it's easy to forget the reliance of modern agriculture on non-renewable energy sources, adding to the problems of global warming and ozone destruction. Producing, transporting, processing and marketing food have all come to depend heavily on fuel and energy.

We're told that cutting out chemicals would make our food more expensive, but it's a price many more people are prepared to pay for ensuring the future of our environment and the health of our children.

Hidden Costs of the CAP

The Common Agricultural Policy keeps food prices artificially high by subsidising big, wealthy growers. The latest scandal is that many are now also paid *not* to farm. Europe's failed attempt to make agriculture more green and at the same time cut over-production – the set-aside scheme – means farmers are paid for leaving part of their land unfarmed. But instead of using fewer chemicals, many farmers use more on the rest of their land to keep up levels of production.

Redirecting more support to truly environmentally-friendly agriculture and small producers is a challenge the European Union faces.

CUTTING THE CHEMICALS

Many of us are understandably worried about the chemicals that are sprayed on our food and the damage intensive agriculture does to our environment. But is enough being done to cut farming's chemical dependency? In Sweden, farmers have cut pesticide usage by 75 per cent in 10 years. That's because their policy has the support of the government, farmers and consumers. In the UK we have no such national policy.

Some retailers have backed schemes based on integrated pest management or integrated crop management – IPM or ICM as they are known. Rather than relying totally on chemical pest control these schemes integrate more 'natural' methods such as the use of natural predators and pheromones to deter pests. Supermarkets have teamed up with farmers to agree which pesticides can be used.

It's good PR for the supermarkets, and certainly a move towards fewer chemicals used on our food is welcome. However, these schemes still permit many toxic pesticides which can damage the environment, and in some cases go little further than reinforcing the importance of compliance with existing legal requirements. Critics say the retailers' promotion of such schemes as an assurance of safe and environmentally-friendly fresh produce can seriously mislead consumers. And what adds to this lack of reassurance is the supermarkets' refusal to make public not only what they do and do not permit but also the results of their own testing for pesticide residues.

Only organic agriculture goes the whole way and cuts out any use of artificial pesticides and chemicals. Its standards are laid down in law and systems of monitoring are open to public scrutiny. But even here the UK lags way behind other European countries in helping farmers change to organic agriculture. Consumers are demanding more and more organic produce. In 1987 we spent just £40 million on organic food; by 1994 this had risen to over £150 million. The outlook is rosy, yet UK organic farmers still get the lowest Government support in Europe. Little wonder that 70 per cent of organic produce presently sold in the UK is imported from other countries.

Choosing Organic

If you choose organic food you can be sure not only that you're avoiding any possible pesticide residues but that the way in which the food has been produced places greater emphasis on animal welfare and helps to protect the health of the environment.

Why Buy Organic?

83 per cent of organic food consumers say they buy organic to avoid pesticide residues

75 per cent agree it is kinder to the environment

70 per cent are worried about intensive rearing of animals

68 per cent say it tastes better

40 per cent buy it to support local farms

36 per cent are worried about BSE

Source: Health Which? April 1997, Consumers' Association.

Organic agriculture relies on crop rotation and natural fertilisers to maintain healthy soil, rather than on chemicals. And it's not just fruit, veg and cereals which are grown organically – an increasing number of farm animals are kept organically, supplying shops with organic free-range eggs, milk and meat. Animal welfare is a priority: their diet must be natural and wholesome, and the routine use of drugs and antibiotics is banned.

It sounds idyllic – but how can you be sure that organic food lives up to these standards? You may see food described as 'traditional', 'natural' or 'environmentally friendly', but the only description which is guaranteed by law is 'organic'. In addition, all producers of organic food must be registered and regularly inspected.

The United Kingdom Register of Organic Food Standards (UKROFS) ensures that European-wide laws are kept, and approves the various bodies which register organic farmers and processors. In the UK these registering bodies are:

The Soil Association
Organic Farmers and Growers
Organic Food Federation
Biodynamic Agricultural Association
Scottish Organic Producers Association
Irish Organic Farmers and Growers Association

You may see their logos on organic produce.

For processed foods you may need to look a little more carefully at the label, as not all ingredients may be organic. Foods can be made with up to 5 per cent non-organic ingredients and still be labelled organic. It's also OK for organic foods to contain only 70 per cent organic ingredients, though the label must state the precise percentage.

Some ingredients are not permitted in organic foods. These include genetically-modified organisms or ingredients that have been irradiated. These same standards apply to imported organic foods.

Where to Find Organic Food

- **Some supermarkets** – Not all supermarkets stock organic food – you won't find any organic food in Marks & Spencer or organic fruit and veg in ASDA or Somerfield. Even in other stores the selection can vary between branches, and in some the choice may be limited.
- **Organic supermarkets** – Two organic supermarket chains – Out of This World (in Bristol, Nottingham and Newcastle) and Planet Organic (in London with plans to expand) – stock organic produce.
- **Box schemes** – You can now have organic food delivered to your door by an increasing number of home delivery or 'box' schemes, some of which supply direct from farm to home. The Soil Association provides a list.
- **Farm shops, independent retailers, mail-order suppliers** – check the Soil Association's list for your nearest supplier.

DOES ORGANIC FOOD TASTE BETTER?

Its supporters say organic food definitely tastes better. In part this may be due to different varieties of crops that are grown, but there is evidence that the use of fertilisers in conventional farming means some vegetables absorb more water, which may make them less tasty. In addition, organic food is usually minimally processed and contains no artificial ingredients.

Organic Food: Good for Men

Eating organic food may be good for fathers. A small-scale Danish study of organic farmers and others who live mainly on organic foods found that these men had nearly double the sperm count of the national average.

Shh, It's a Secret

A report showing that fruit and vegetables grown organically contain higher levels of vitamins and minerals was suppressed by MAFF for four years. The Government-funded research was initially marked 'confidential'. Later it had been made 'available to the food industry' and a single copy put in the MAFF library.

The research, which looked at 30 samples of fruit and vegetables bought in supermarkets and health food stores, found significant nutritional differences between some organic and non-organic produce. Organic apples and tomatoes tended to be richer in vitamins than non-organic, though carrots and cabbage showed few significant differences.[4]

Food Miles

'Before you finish eating your breakfast this morning you've depended on half the world,' so said Martin Luther King. Few of us give much thought to where our food comes from and who produces it, but long gone are the days when Farmer Giles took his produce down the road to the local market. Now much fruit and veg is air-freighted halfway round the world. Even food grown in the UK may travel up and down the country from farm to wholesaler to a central supermarket distribution centre and then back to local supermarkets. In the UK we import more food than we export, to the tune of £6.7 billion. Only 25 per cent of the apples we eat are home-grown, yet in France 90 per cent of apples eaten are produced there – despite the fact that many would say ours are tastier. Yet we've grubbed up over half of English orchards since the 1950s and now import apples from Europe, New Zealand, South Africa, Chile and the US.

When we reach the checkout the price we pay for our groceries doesn't include the costs of the air pollution from lorries and planes that are adding to global warming and ozone depletion. Neither do we pay for pesticide poisoning and pollution from intensive agriculture; or the ecological damage from growing unsuitable crops in developing countries; or the declining rural communities and unemployment in the UK as small farmers and farm workers are forced out of business because they cannot compete with cheap imports.

The Long-distance Yoghurt

Take one pot of yoghurt and add up all the miles that its ingredients, its packaging and the final product have travelled. That's what one German study did – the strawberries came from Poland, the corn and wheat flour from the Netherlands, sugar beet from East Germany, the label and aluminium foil covers over 300 km away. Only the glass jar and milk were produced locally. Add up all the miles travelled and all in all a 'theoretical' lorry would have to travel 540 miles just to produce one 150g pot of yoghurt. Multiply that for a whole shopping trolley and it's easy to see how our diet burns up diesel and belches out nitrogen oxides, sulphur dioxide and other toxic gases into the air.

THINK GLOBAL, BUY LOCAL

One of the ways round the problem of food miles is to think global and buy local, either from small local shops and markets or direct from farms. In many areas 'box schemes' offer seasonal organic fruit and veg from local farmers delivered to your door (contact the Soil Association for details). By buying local fresh, seasonal food whenever it is available, local farmers are kept in business, food is fresher and tastier with less need for packaging, less fuel is used and there's less need for post-harvest pesticide treatments to keep the food fresh during transport and storage. One of the pleasures of eating fruit and vegetables in season is rediscovering their real taste. Out of season produce may look good but its taste can disappoint.

Down on the Farm

With scares about mad cow disease, *E. coli* and salmonella food poisoning and concerns over the way farm animals are treated, meat has been under the spotlight as never before. While more people are becoming vegetarian, many more are demi-vegetarians, occasional rather than everyday meat eaters. And many who continue to eat meat are becoming more discerning. More and more of us want to know if the chicken that laid our breakfast egg was free-range, whether the Sunday roast has been pumped full of antibiotics and hormones or what we are really eating when we bite into a sausage, burger or other processed meat product. And it's not always so easy to tell.

We bring up our children with images of happy animals down on the farm – images that have changed little over the past century. It's the same cosy rural image that the food industry would like us to believe. But the reality is often very different. The production of meat, eggs and milk has changed considerably in the last 50 years. The emphasis has been on producing more and more while cutting costs. As a result we certainly have a plentiful supply of cheap meat – but at what cost?

BSE has taught us that we tamper with nature at our peril. It's fairly certain that the feeding of sheep remains to cattle allowed the sheep disease scrapie to jump species and cause the devastating outbreak of BSE in cattle which has now been linked to CJD in humans. So where did it all go wrong?

The Modern Meat Machine

The pressure to produce more meat at cheaper prices has led to intensive systems of food production where, typically, animal welfare has been compromised, there is often a reliance on the routine use of drugs and feed can be a far cry from the natural diet of farm animals.

BATTERY HENS

Seventy-five per cent of all British eggs are produced by battery hens. Thirty million of these poor creatures are kept in row upon row of battery cages in sheds of typically 30,000 to 100,000 birds. Each cage houses five hens, each with less than the area of an A4 piece of paper. The artificial lighting is kept on for 17 hours a day to promote greater egg-laying. The birds can perform little of their natural behaviour and their lack of movement causes weak bones which often break. Birds are often debeaked – the tip of their beaks are cut with a hot blade – to prevent cannibalism in the stressed and overcrowded conditions.

Their diet is also a far cry from what they would eat naturally. Included in their rations could be meat and bonemeal from other slaughtered animals, fish meal and feather and blood meal from poultry slaughterhouses. And along with this typically comes a regular dose of antibiotics and other medicines, together with yellow colourings to ensure the egg yolk is a deep healthy-looking golden yellow.

BROILER CHICKENS

Over 600 million broiler chickens a year are reared in windowless sheds, typically in flocks of 10–20,000 birds. They are specially bred to be fast-growing which, encouraged by growth-promoting drugs, means that they are slaughtered at just 6–7 weeks old. Yet in their short lives many suffer bone deformities.

TURKEYS

Most turkeys are reared intensively, crowded in huge densely-packed sheds to be fattened up in time for the Christmas market. Turkeys find it hard to adapt to such unnatural indoor rearing and often react by attacking each other. For this reason they have the tips of their beaks removed with a red-hot blade, which can cause lasting suffering. Because turkeys have been bred to have unnaturally large amounts of breast meat they are predisposed towards leg injuries and lameness and they are also too top heavy to mate naturally. Females have to be artificially inseminated.

PIGS

There are around 7–8 million pigs in the UK. Pigs naturally prefer to live in family groups and to build large nests for their piglets. Although over a fifth of British pork is now 'outdoor reared' (*see 'Animal Welfare-friendly Meat, page 174*), intensive indoor systems are still the norm.

During their 16-week pregnancy Britain's sows are often kept indoors in sow stalls or tethers. The sow stall is a metal-barred stall which is so narrow that the sow can't turn around or associate with other pigs. In a tether stall the pig is tied to the concrete floor by a chain. Tethering causes much distress as well as lameness, sores and hip problems, with animals frequently exhibiting repetitive behaviour symptoms. Campaigning by animal welfare organisations now means that sow stalls and tethers are being phased out and will be banned in the UK in 1999. However in many other European countries which export pork, such as Denmark, Holland and Ireland, sow stalls are still the norm and only tethers will be prohibited, but even then not until 2006.

There are plans to ban restrictive farrowing crates in which 80 per cent of British sows are forced to give birth, ostensibly to prevent sows squashing their piglets. Piglets are prematurely taken away from their mothers at just 3–4 weeks so the sow can be made pregnant again. Overcrowded pens can make piglets aggressive and lead to tail-biting common behaviour. Many farmers prevent this by tail docking – a painful mutilation.

DAIRY COWS

The modern dairy cow is arguably the most overworked of farm animals, producing levels of milk far in excess of her natural capacity. The natural lifespan of a dairy cow is up to 20 years, but typically by the age of five she is usually so worn out she is usually sent for slaughter. Distended and heavy udders often lead to lameness and mastitis, a painful infection of the udder, which means treatment with antibiotics. Milk from treated cows should not be sold for consumption, but the residues of antibiotics which from time to time turn up in milk show that this is not always the case.

Daisy's diet has also changed dramatically. Most of us thought cows ate grass, but BSE has brought home the unpalatable truth of cows fed recycled animal remains along with fish meal, soya beans and other high-protein foods which are not part of their natural diet. In winter many are confined indoors with solid concrete or slatted floors, which adds to the strain on their legs and the incidence of lameness.

In spite of all this, scientists are still looking for ways to boost milk production even higher. The genetically-engineered milk-boosting hormone BST (bovine somatotropin), already in use in the US, is banned in Europe until the end of the century – but this ban is being strongly challenged (*see page 192*). Regular injections increase the amount of milk produced but also increase the pressures on the modern dairy cow even further.

CALVES

Calves are typically separated from their mothers soon after birth, which is distressing for both mother and calf. Many are destined for the veal trade and sent to market when just a few days old. Veal crates have been illegal in the UK since 1990, but until the ban on the export of British beef due to BSE was introduced calves continued to be exported to veal farms in France and Holland. At the peak of the trade, over 1,000 British calves were exported every day to be reared for three to six months in narrow wooden crates in the dark, unable to turn around and fed on milk liquids low in iron to develop the 'white' meat of veal. The trade is likely to resume once the ban is lifted. In the UK veal is reared more humanely. Though they are kept indoors, calves are kept in groups with bedding on the floor.

SHEEP

Typically sheep are the least intensively reared farm animals, but even they have not escaped pressures to produce more. Sheep are bred to encourage twins and now there are pressures for all-year-round British lamb. This would mean keeping lambs indoors eating feed concentrates and growth promoters.

ANIMAL TRANSPORT

Protests against live animal exports have highlighted the conditions many animals face while transported on long journeys to the continent or to slaughterhouses. Animal welfare campaigners want to see animals slaughtered in local abattoirs, journeys limited to a maximum of eight hours; they also want the practice of exporting live animals outlawed. Some animals such as adult cattle and sheep can still be transported for up to 30 hours under EC rules.

SLAUGHTER

Humane slaughter gives the impression of animals put quietly to sleep. The reality is rather different. The law requires animals to be stunned into unconsciousness and to remain unconscious until they are dead, but in poorly run slaughter houses this may not happen and some animals may regain consciousness while bleeding to death.

By 1991 all abattoirs should have met new hygiene standards under rules from Brussels. But by 1997 only half of the British abattoirs were operating to these standards. Two hundred of the 469 are 'exempt' because they normally slaughter less than 1,000 animals a year, while 45 were still operating under 'temporary derogations' which have allowed abattoirs to avoid upgrading to EU standards. This may have exacerbated problems of *E. coli* food poisoning (*see page 184*).

Love Me Tender

The traditional way to tenderise meat is to hang it, but it's expensive, partly because of the weight loss due to drip. Then came the idea of injecting animals with meat-tenderising enzymes before they were killed. Thankfully this has been outlawed for its cruelty. Now butchers have a new way of turning the tough tender. Tenderising machines, which cut the connective tissue and sinews of meat with closely spaced blades, offer butchers a legal and cheap way of improving the 'quality' of meat. And, importantly for the butcher, it leaves no tell-tale signs, so unsuspecting customers will happily pay over the odds.

Designer Daisy

Dairy cows that give skimmed milk, milk fortified with healthy fish oils and butter that spreads straight from the fridge? Have the cows gone mad? Well not the cows, but maybe the scientists who are hoping to persuade us that such 'designer' dairy foods are good for our health.

The secret, it seems, lies in the cows' diet. By adding fish to her diet, Daisy can produce milk rich in omega-3, a fatty acid which can help to prevent heart disease. Meanwhile, feeding dehusked oats apparently produces the semi-skimmed milk, while for spreadable butter rapeseed oil does the trick. And it seems poor Daisy can be programmed to provide any of the new products and switched between them.

But with fish stocks under threat and BSE to remind us of the effects of tinkering with cows' diets, these latest 'designer foods' could get a cool reception from consumers.

You Are What You Eat

Much modern meat production relies on the use of antibiotics, growth-promoting substances and other additives which are often routinely added to feed. Residues of these substances can sometimes turn up in our food.

HORMONES AND OTHER ILLEGAL GROWTH-PROMOTERS

In their bid to make animals grow larger faster, farmers have been known to resort to the illegal use of growth-promoting substances. In Europe the use of steroid hormones in meat production is banned, although this has been challenged by the US, where they are permitted, on the grounds that banning them is a barrier to free trade. Currently US meat, produced with hormones, is not permitted, to be imported into Europe. Other illegal growth-promoters include clenbuterol, which is used to increase lean meat. It's known to have caused several deaths of beef consumers in Spain. Tests by consumer organisations[1] found a small number of samples of UK steak and beef liver contaminated with these illegal growth-promoters, although far less than found in some other countries. There need to be tougher controls and greater sanctions for illegal use of meat hormones. But cleaning up this illegal underworld has not proved easy – a Belgian vet who vowed to stamp out illegal meat hormones was shot dead in 1995.

ANTIBIOTICS

Antibiotics are routinely fed to intensively-reared farm animals along with their daily rations – not because they are ill but to make them grow faster and to prevent weight-loss infections which are mainly due to the crowded, enclosed conditions in which they are kept. Traces of drug residues can sometimes turn up in meat and milk, and there are now concerns that their use is encouraging the growth of resistant super-bugs which are affecting human health (*see 'Superbugs', page 171*). In 1997 the Consumers' Association and other European consumer organisations tested meat for antibiotic residues. In the UK 7 per cent of turkeys and 4 per cent of pork contained residues; the worst problem was in the Republic of Ireland, where 17 per cent of pork was found to contain antibiotics.[2]

COLOURINGS

Ever wondered how that battery egg yolk was so yellow, or that farmed fish so pink? The answer is likely to be colourings in the chicken or fish feed. One colour, canthaxanthin, is still permitted in animal feed although it is banned as a direct additive in food for humans because it can damage the eyes.

VITAMINS

The use of vitamin A in animal feed as a growth-promoter has led to high concentrations being found in liver. Now the Department of Health warns pregnant women to avoid eating liver – as high levels of vitamin A can damage the developing baby.

Superbugs

There are now fears that the routine use of antibiotics in farming may be undermining the effectiveness of antibiotics used for human health. So much so that the World Health Organization has called for measures to reduce the reservoir of resistant bacteria – both in medical and farming practices.

In the UK, since 1968, antibiotics needed for human health are not allowed to be given to animals. But there is now evidence that cross-resistance from animal to human drugs may be occurring. For example, resistance to the widely used antibiotic avoparcin – used mainly for pigs and chickens, but also for dairy cows, calves and beef cattle – may be transferring to one of our most important human antibiotics, vancomycin. While avoparcin is still in use in the UK, Germany and Denmark have banned it. Sweden has gone even further: It banned all antibiotics from animal feed in 1986. Today Sweden claims to be Europe's main producer of salmonella-free chickens. Ironically, while these European countries are promoting high animal welfare and health standards, their tough stance is being challenged under European Union rules, which make it difficult for individual countries to step out of line with others with lower standards.

As resistance to drugs increases, so do the superbugs. In 1995 over 87 per cent of one particular form of salmonella, which has transferred to humans from the farm, was resistant to five common antibiotics. In addition, imported chickens have been found to contain *Campylobacter* bacteria that are resistant to the antibiotic ciproflacin. The drug is used to treat humans, but in some countries it's also used to boost growth in chickens.

To keep within maximum residue limits (MRLs), farmers must stop giving animals antibiotics a certain time before slaughter. But as residues do sometimes turn up in meat and milk, it's clear that this does not always happen.

This Little Piggy Went to Market

Residues of the antibiotic sulphonamide in pigs have been a problem for some time – in 1995 high levels of sulphonamide were found in 1.3 per cent of pigs' kidneys tested. Its use to treat pig respiratory problems has been growing. Lack of careful controls also means that some feed which should have been free of the antibiotic was contaminated.[3]

Going Wild

If you're wary of beef and bored with pork and chicken, why not go a little wild with buffalo, kangaroo, ostrich, wild boar or even crocodile? For the more adventurous eater, restaurants and some supermarkets are now offering a range of these 'new' meats. Not only might they tickle our tastebuds – at a price – they might also be good for us as they tend to be lower in fat than most other meats. However, animal welfare campaigners say that their wild instincts make them unsuitable for farming.

Fish Farming

Salmon and trout are no longer the luxuries they once were, thanks to the huge growth of fish farming. But it's not all such good news. Farmed fish are not only less healthy and therefore reliant on a cocktail of chemicals, they are also less healthy for us. Farmed salmon tend to be fattier than their wild cousins – they just don't have the room to swim, nor are they fed their natural diet – all of which means their taste fails to match that of their wild counterparts.

However, the most serious effect of fish farming is its impact on the environment and the other sea creatures living close to fish farms. Many beautiful coastal regions such as the Scottish lochs are now facing serious environmental problems from fish farming and the chemicals it uses.

Some fish is now farmed to higher environmental standards, using less chemicals and with reduced stocking densities. Such fish will certainly cost more, but it's a price worth paying to protect our marine heritage.

CHEMICAL COCKTAIL

Sea lice infestation and other diseases are often rife in the confines of the floating cages, and a cocktail of toxic chemicals are used to treat the fish. Spot checks have found toxic residues in the fish.

- **Ivermectin** – for years this neurotoxin was banned on fish farms, although its illegal use went on unchecked. Now, because of industry pressure it is being authorised on increasing numbers of Scottish fish farms. The chemical can be a poison to shell fish and other sea creatures living on the sea bed, as well as being a risk to human health. Despite assurances that fish shouldn't contain the chemical, Government spot checks in 1994 found residues in 10 per cent of fish.[4] In 1995, 11 out of 359 were above the level triggering investigation, yet prosecutions for illegal use are rare.
- **Dichlorvos** – also used to treat sea lice. On the Government's 'Red List' of most dangerous substances. Known to be toxic to other sea creatures even at low doses. Residues of dichlorvos have been found in farmed salmon.
- **Malachite green** – used as a fungicide. Known to potentially damage the developing foetus. Is a carcinogen. In 1996 the Ministry of Agriculture, Fisheries and Food (MAFF)'s Veterinary Medicines Directorate found unexpected (and unacceptable) residues of malachite green in trout.
- **Antibiotics** – routinely added to much fish feed.
- **Dyes** – added to the feed to ensure fish look pink. Can include canthaxanthin, which is banned for direct use in human food but which can turn up in farmed fish – and you won't find anything on the label to tell you.

Plenty More Fish in the Sea?

Fish stocks worldwide are under threat from over-fishing. But fish does not just end up on your dinner plate. Almost 30 per cent of the world's catch, some 20 million tonnes annually, is used for feeding pigs or chickens or even farmed fish. Fish is also used in fertilisers and for making fish oils.

Animal Welfare-friendly Meat

Television programmes have brought the secrets of intensive animal husbandry – whether battery cages for debeaked hens, veal crates for young calves or tethered sows – into our living rooms. More and more people are concerned about the way in which their meat is produced. Two out of three people say they are concerned about the welfare of animals raised on farms and that they would like to see more information on food labels.[5] Many, especially the young, are turning towards vegetarianism, but there are also increasing numbers of consumers who are prepared to eat eggs, dairy products and meat so long as they can be sure that the animals are reared to higher standards of animal welfare. But how can you tell?

Supermarkets stock eggs and sell meat with cosy-sounding descriptions such as 'traditional', 'free-range', 'heritage' and 'farm assured', often with images of picture book farmyards and idyllic rural landscapes. Such descriptions certainly conjure up images of contented animals enjoying a kinder, more natural way of farming, but how can we be sure? The truth may not be so idyllic. The problem for the consumer is that there are few legal controls on such descriptions and it can be difficult to assess just what improvements many such schemes offer. In some cases schemes have more to do with PR gloss than with real differences in the way meat is produced.

WHAT THE LABELS MEAN

Organic Meat

Organic standards are the Rolls Royce of agriculture. Meat raised to organic standards must meet strict standards which have the additional reassurance of being enshrined by law. These affect meat production from the farm to the retailer, covering animal welfare, feed and medication, transport and slaughter procedures. The main certifying body is UKROFS (the UK Register of Organic Food Standards). Its standards guarantee that animal feed must be organically grown and pesticide-free; growth-promoters and the routine use of drugs are not allowed, and animals must be able to graze outdoors. Battery cages for hens and farrowing crates for sows are not permitted, neither are debeaking of hens or tail docking of piglets. Standards also cover animal transport and slaughterhouses. Some supermarkets now sell organic meat and there are an increasing number of specialist butchers and retailers, some mail order. The Soil Association provides a list (*see page 219*).

The Real Meat Company

The Real Meat Company supplies quality meat and meat products which have been produced to its own Codes of Diet and Welfare which includes transport and slaughter. This offers higher standards than conventionally reared meat, although the key difference from organically produced meat is that the Real Meat Company standards do not insist that animal feed is organic or guaranteed pesticide-free.

Free-range

This term is used to describe some meat and eggs. But the only legal definitions apply to eggs and poultry. There are no legal definitions of free-range for meat such as pork, lamb or beef, so labels for these meats claiming 'free-range' may be meaningless unless there are published definitions and, preferably, an independent certifying system.

Free-range Poultry

Although enshrined by law, free-range is a really confusing term when used for poultry – in fact there are three sets of standards laid down by the EC – **'Free-range'**, **'traditional free-range'** and **'free-range total freedom'**. As with the eggs, minimum free-range standards are set much lower than consumers typically expect. Only 'free-range total freedom' standards provide hens with complete outdoor access – but even these are permitted to be routinely fed antibiotics and other drugs. Birds reared to traditional free-range and free-range total freedom standards are slower growing and likely to be tastier. **Corn-fed** chickens, as their name suggests, have been largely fed on corn (maize), providing them with their characteristic yellow colour. It's intended to improve the flavour, though this also depends on the breed of the bird and whether it is free-range.

And don't be misled into thinking that poultry described as **extensive indoor** or **barn reared** is anything very special. While these do fall into the over-wide legal EC definition of free-range, the way they are raised is only marginally better than that for broiler chickens.

Outdoor Reared Pork

This gives the impression of pigs in fields, but typically after a period outdoors young pigs are brought into open barns to be fattened.

Farm Assured Meat

After the BSE scandal, retailers have been keen to restore consumer confidence with such labels. The National Farm Assurance Scheme covers cattle, sheep and pigs, but this only provides an audit trail, which means that meat can be traced back to its source. It does not offer a significant improvement on current livestock practices. Only the pigs scheme is monitored by MAFF inspectors.

'Traditional' or 'Traditionally Matured' Beef and Lamb

This labelling can give the impression of improved farming practices. But in reality much of the meat described in this way will not be reared very differently from the vast majority of UK-produced beef and lamb.

Heritage

This is used to describe a range of Safeway's meat which includes free-range chicken, outdoor reared pork and traditionally matured beef and lamb.

Freedom Foods

Launched by the RSPCA in 1994, the Freedom Foods scheme aims to certify meat produced to the RSPCA's 'Five Freedoms' standards. It has been welcomed as a step in the right direction, outlawing as it does some of the worst practices of intensive farming. But it has been criticised for failing to set higher standards. Eggs can bear the Freedom Foods symbol even when they have been laid by hens which have never experienced natural light. Also permitted are farrowing crates, debeaking of chickens, tail docking for piglets and gas-stunning of pigs in slaughter houses. However, live transport for over eight hours is banned. In response to its critics the RSPCA argues that setting standards higher would be counterproductive to encouraging farmers towards more humane practices.

Eggsplanations

Farm Fresh or Country Fresh Eggs
Despite the words and often pretty images on the egg box, these are eggs laid by battery hens. Yet even supermarket managers can be confused. A survey by Compassion in World Farming found that over a quarter of local store managers did not know the difference between 'free-range' eggs and those marked 'farm fresh' or 'country

---

fresh'. Only the Co-op labels its battery eggs as 'intensively pro-duced' and refuses to carry farmyard pictures giving idyllic images of a chicken's life.

Barn and Perchery Eggs

This is supposedly an improvement on the battery system as hens are not kept in cages. In theory the hens have more room to move around, but in practice they have no access to the outdoors and are often so crowded that they become aggressive and fight for food and space. Debeaking is routine and their diet is typically no im-provement on that of a battery hen.

Free-range Eggs

Buying free-range eggs eases our conscience, but should it? Euro-pean Union standards for free-range eggs are pathetically poor. Free-range hens must have continuous access to the outdoors, but in reality there is no limit to the number of birds that can be kept in a 'free-range' chicken house. The number may commonly exceed 7,000 birds, of which only a small percentage manage to venture outside. For those that do, the outside area may be barren and un-attractive. It's also widespread practice to expose free-range birds to the stress of extended daylight using artificial light to encourage greater egg-laying. There are no standards to ensure an additive- or drug-free diet, and free-range hens usually have their beaks cut too.

There's a world of difference between the minimum standards required for free-range and the best free-range systems. These allow no more than about 300 birds in a flock, in small movable houses which allow regular fresh pasture and genuine freedom to range. They are fed a natural, wholesome diet free of drugs and ad-ditives and often produced to organic standards. Eggs of this stan-dard are more likely to be found in specialist or wholefood shops rather than supermarkets. Read the labels carefully, not just for what they say but also what they don't say. Once you've found a supplier of naturally free-range eggs you'll taste the difference too.

Freedom Food Eggs

These must meet the RSPCA's 'freedom food' standards, but in practice the standards fall short of even the low ones set for free-range eggs. Beak-clipping is still permitted as are antibiotics and colourings in the diet.

Organic Eggs

These must meet organic standards laid down by an organic certifying body. Eggs must meet the best free-range standards, with easy and continuous access to outdoors. Flocks must be of fewer than 500 birds, and beak clipping is not permitted. At least 70 per cent of the birds' diet must be organically produced and free from antibiotics, animal waste and protein, and yolk-colouring dyes.

Four Grain Eggs

Producers say hens must be fed only a 'natural diet' free from animal protein, colourings and medicines, but you can't assume the eggs are free-range – their diet may be healthier than the average hen's but they are still kept in the barn system.

Banned Drugs Found in Eggs

Government tests have found that one in eight eggs contains traces of the banned drug nicarbazin. This drug is routinely added to feed to control parasites in broiler chickens, but it is not permitted for egg-laying hens. Similar problems have been found with another drug, dimetridazole, which is fed to turkeys but not permitted for chickens. MAFF's Veterinary Medicines Directorate say it's an on-going problem, most likely caused by cross-contamination of feed during processing, transport or on the farm.

We're told that the residues pose no threat to consumers, but the results highlight continuing food safety problems within the animal feed industry. Even buying free-range eggs won't guarantee eggs free from drug residues. The survey found just as many free-range eggs were contaminated as intensively-produced ones. Despite their 'green' and healthier image, free-range hens can be fed the same diet as battery hens, including the routine addition of medication and yolk dyes.

Are Brown Eggs Healthier than White?

Somehow the idea has grown up that brown eggs are healthier, tastier and more natural than white eggs. But there's no truth in this myth – the difference in colour is due solely to the different varieties of hen. But because of this negative image of white eggs, virtually all eggs, whether produced in a battery or free-range system, are now brown.

How Fresh Are 'Fresh' Eggs?

The fresher the egg, the tastier and safer it is – if an egg is infected with salmonella the bacteria will grow to more dangerous levels in the days and sometimes weeks before an egg may be eaten. But how can you tell when your egg was laid? Eggs should come with a 'best before' date, but there's no legal limit on when that should be. In fact it can be up to 28 days after the eggs were laid. Some may come labelled with a 'packing date' but don't be misled – this isn't the same as the date the eggs were laid – in practice it can be anything up to 10 days after laying. So that 'fresh' egg could in fact be several weeks old. Only a handful of better quality egg producers mark their eggs with a laying date.

Funny Farm

It's a stressful life being a battery chicken, but those clever boffins are doing their best to find a way of making it more tolerable. Researchers say that regular stroking, a good selection of toys to play with and watching television could help to relieve fear and aggression and boost growth and resistance to disease. There's no suggestion from the researchers that they'd be better off as free-range chickens, but lucky battery hens may be allowed to watch images of green fields on the big screen.

As for stressed-out pigs, scientists are now working on removing their stress-susceptibility by genetic engineering. It's good news for the meat trade, which reports – no, not happy pigs and farmers living in gentle harmony – but 'a 0.5 per cent improvement in pigmeat water-holding capacity ... worth about £1 per pig.'

The Madness of BSE

The Government handling of BSE (Bovine Spongiform Encephalopathy) has been a scandal and a fiasco – a sad catalogue of incompetence, cover-up and collusion. While those campaigning for reform of UK food policies have long argued that the links between farmers, the food industry and Government were too close for comfort, the BSE crisis has shown the world that in the UK public health comes a pretty poor second to shoring up the food and farming industries.

Little by little we've seen more and more bits of beef banned from our food. First to be banned in 1989 – three years after the first cases of BSE were identified – were brain, spinal cord, thymus, tonsils, spleen and intestine. As Government scientists have had to admit that they don't know exactly what is 'safe', other parts of the animal have been added to the list. The ban on bones from the spine was extended to their use in mechanically recovered meat (MRM) in December 1995. In making the announcement of its ban, the then Agriculture Minister Douglas Hogg said that he was pleased to be acting 'promptly' – yet MAFF had let MRM slip through the net for six years even though it was known that the spinal cord, one of the most infective parts of the animal, was not always properly removed from spine bones. Tail vertebrae have been excluded from the ban, so oxtail is still on sale. The whole head, but not the tongue, was banned in 1996.

After reassuring us that these bans meant there was absolutely no longer any risk to human health, MAFF finally admitted that there had been failures and some banned offals could have got into the human food chain after 1989. Inspectors found that nearly half of slaughterhouses were failing to remove the spinal cord from cattle vertebrae. This was a clear breach of Government regulations, five years after they were introduced in 1990. And even then, spot checks by Government inspectors were still finding spinal cord attached to carcasses in some cases. In the summer of 1996 environmental health officers in Birmingham reported finding banned offal in meat on sale to the public.

Cases of BSE are declining but it will take many years yet for it to be fully eradicated. In the meantime, 14 people have died of the new variant form of Creuzfeldt-Jakob disease which has been linked to BSE. In addition thousands of cattle have been slaughtered, businesses and livelihoods have been threatened and taxpayers will foot the £3.3 billion bill to sort out the mess created by inadequate action at an earlier stage.

Even now, over 10 years after BSE was first identified, many questions remain unanswered, particularly the most important question of all: is beef safe to eat? The answer is that it is impossible to be absolutely, 100 per cent sure. Certainly the risk will be lower now than prior to 1989.

Some scientists say that it is probably too late for most adults to start worrying about eating beef now. We may well have already eaten quite large quantities of possibly-infected meat, and therefore the advantage of stopping eating beef now is relatively small. For children, who have eaten relatively little, it's argued there may be greater advantages in stopping now.

You can reduce any potential risk by choosing muscle meat such as steaks and joints rather than pies, burgers, sausages and other processed meat products, and by choosing organic beef from fully certified herds. But if you really want to be absolutely sure, the only way is to avoid all beef and beef ingredients (see 'Hidden Beef', page 11).

QUESTIONS ABOUT BSE ANSWERED

- **Can cooking destroy the BSE agent?** – No. The temperature required to kill the BSE agent is far higher than that used in cooking.
- **Is milk safe?** – Milk is not thought to transmit BSE, but as a precaution milk from cows with suspected BSE must be destroyed. In 1997 the EU's Scientific Veterinary Committee concluded that there is no evidence that milk from cows transmits BSE. It also stated that there was no evidence that rennet (from cows' stomachs, used to make cheese) or whey protein from milk is a risk, although it called for more research.
- **Is non-British beef safer?** – The UK has by far the biggest BSE problem in the world. While small numbers of cases have been confirmed in other countries, many of these are linked to the import of UK cattle or cattle feed. But it can be difficult if not impossible to tell where beef comes from as it's not obligatory for food labels to tell you the country of origin of meat. In 1996 fast-food chains rushed to reassure customers that they did not use British beef, though some have now reversed this decision; in any case, generally it is impossible to know where meat or meat ingredients in foods have come from. Ask your butcher, supermarket or food manufacturer, if you want to know.
- **Is gelatin safe?** – Gelatin is made from the bones or hides of mainly, but not exclusively, cattle. It's used in many foods such as sweets, yoghurts, desserts and pork pies as well as capsules for vitamin pills and medicines. MAFF says that gelatin is safe because it is heated and treated with chemicals which would reduce the infectivity of any BSE agent, and British bovine material is now banned from its production.
- **Liver?** – Unlike many other offals, liver is not banned – even though the BSE agent has occasionally been found in liver at moderate to low levels. No meat from infected animals *should* get into the human food chain, but there has been evidence of animals with early signs of the disease being sent for slaughter and not being rejected by abattoir inspectors. If you're worried, don't eat it.
- **Bonemeal?** – Bonemeal is banned as a fertiliser on ground where it might be eaten by ruminants, but there's no restrictions on using it in

your garden where pets or children could come into contact with it. The safest advice is not to use it, or, if you do, to wear gloves, goggles and a mask.

- **Offal from calves under six months** – this has not been prohibited from human food, as these calves are too young to have developed the disease, it is argued.
- **Is organic beef safer?** – Buying organic beef cannot guarantee that the animal was free from BSE but it can reduce the risk. Organic cattle are mainly fed grass; Soil Association standards banned the feeding of all animal material, including fish meal, to cattle and sheep in 1983. There have been a few cases of BSE within organic herds but at much lower levels than on conventional farms. It's thought these were animals bought in from conventional farms.

Food Poisoning

The number of reported cases of food poisoning in Britain has increased at an alarming rate. Since 1980 the number of notified cases of food poisoning has risen nine-fold to reach 90,000 in 1995. While this may be due in part to increased reporting, experts agree that the rise is real and extremely worrying. What's more, tougher, more virulent bugs are appearing. A virulent form of *E. coli* known as O157 was the cause of Europe's worst food poisoning outbreak in Scotland in 1996 which killed 19 people (*see 'Coming Clean', page 186*). It can also cause kidney failure, particularly in children. And an increasing number of other common bacteria are becoming resistant to antibiotics.

Campylobacter and salmonella are the most common causes of food poisoning (*see 'Bugs on the Block', page 187*). However, reported cases are just the tip of the iceberg – many more cases of food poisoning go unrecorded if people don't go to their doctor.

With Government health campaigns warning us about kitchen hygiene and the safe storage and cooking of food it's easy to get the impression that it's the housewife who is chiefly to blame for this increase. But while good kitchen hygiene in the home is important (*see 'Kitchen Hygiene', page 189*), the problem has got much more to do with the way that modern food is produced. Intensive production of meat, poultry and eggs, the way that animals are slaughtered and the greater time and distances from the farm to our dinner plates are the ingredients in a recipe for food poisoning disaster. Modern large-scale farming methods have increased the spread of bacteria through contaminated feed and intensive rearing systems. That means there need to be high standards of hygiene all through the food chain. Sadly this is not always the case; for the consumer there is no way of telling whether foods are contaminated.

The only safe way to treat foods, especially meat, eggs and foods made with them, is to assume that there may be a risk of contamination. Edwina Currie was right to draw attention to the problem when she said in 1988 that 'most of British egg production is, sadly, infected' with salmonella, though it was a sad indictment on the Government that she was forced to resign.

And it's questionable whether there have been significant improvements since then. A check of fresh chickens from leading supermarkets and butchers by the Consumers' Association (CA) found that half contained bacteria which could cause food poisoning and many weren't even in a fit state to eat. Thirty-two out of the 90 fresh chickens examined by a top independent poultry expert were judged to be 'unfit for human consumption' because of bruising, infections and contamination. Others had not been properly gutted or bled. Damage or disease can increase the chance of contamination and therefore the risk of food poisoning. The Consumers' Association reported that slaughterhouse inspectors and supermarket quality controllers were clearly failing, in many cases, to weed out such problems.[6]

In separate tests in 1996 the CA[7] tested 160 fresh and frozen chickens bought from supermarkets and butchers. Overall, half the chickens tested had either campylobacter or salmonella bacteria. Salmonella was found in 20 per cent of the chickens – some improvement on the 36 per cent found in 1994. However, campylobacter was found in 37 per cent of the chickens (compared with 41 per cent in 1994).

Thorough cooking should ensure such bacteria are destroyed, but the responsibility for safe food should not rest with the consumer. As the Government's Advisory Committee on the Microbiological Safety of Food has said, it is industry which has the major responsibility for reducing bacterial contamination. While the UK is still arguing about the best way to reduce contamination of chickens, Sweden has largely eliminated the problem, partly by banning the use of antibiotics in chicken feed.

Beef burgers can be another high risk food if not handled and cooked properly. Mincing meat allows any bacteria on the surface of the meat to be distributed throughout the product. One study found *E. coli* 0157 in up to 22 per cent of raw beef products.[8] There have been cases linked to under-cooked burgers from fast food chains. Despite Government advice that burgers should be thoroughly cooked all the way through until the juices run clear, cooking instructions on many shop-bought products are still inadequate. In 1997, six years after the Department of Health's advice, a survey by the Food Commission found many products were still failing to give adequate safety advice.[9]

Coming Clean

In 1996/7 one of the world's worst *E. coli* food poisoning outbreaks led to the deaths of 19 people in central Scotland and affected a further 400. The source of the outbreak was a butchers' shop which had supplied contaminated cooked meat products. The enquiry by Professor Pennington into the disaster says improvements must be made in the way in which meat is sold to the public. Rather than deregulation in food safety, he calls for rigorous enforcement of food safety rules, for the separation of raw meats from cooked meats in butchers' shops and supermarkets, for training of food handlers and for improved standards on farms and in slaughterhouses.

But this isn't the first time there have been calls for better food hygiene standards. It was after the Salmonella-in-eggs affair in 1989 that the Government introduced legislation – the Food Safety

Act 1990 – which promised to clean up British food. But two proposals – for licensing of food premises and mandatory hygiene training for workers – were excluded under pressure from the food industry, and subsequently some temperature control regulations have also been relaxed.

Shh, It's a Secret – Meat Under Wraps

In 1997 the Government was accused of watering down and then suppressing a damning report into hygiene practices in abattoirs which were likely to increase the risk of food poisoning and BSE. Subsequently 19 people died from *E. coli* food poisoning in Scotland.

Hygiene inspectors, who had undertaken the survey in 1996 for the Government's Meat Hygiene Service, fully expected their findings to be published and for their wide-ranging recommendations to be implemented. But by then the BSE crisis was at its height and such a damning report would have further undermined public confidence, already at an all-time low. The Government denied a cover-up but were unable to explain why the report had first been watered down and then suppressed. It was freely available, the Agriculture Minister said, although it seems he had failed to inform anyone of its existence, including Professor Hugh Pennington, who headed the official enquiry into the causes of *E. coli* food poisoning following the deaths in Scotland.

Bugs on the Block

E. Coli

Full name *Escherichia coli*, this bacterium lives in the guts of mammals, including humans. Most types are harmless but some, such as *E. coli* 0157 (also known as VTEC) can cause severe food poisoning. In severe cases it can cause kidney failure and death; as with all food poisoning, the old, young or weak are particularly susceptible. Until 10 years ago it was rare, but its incidence has increased dramatically since then. It is commonly associated with under-cooked meat, particularly meat products from cows such as burgers. Poor hygiene can contaminate meat in slaughterhouses and other meat may be infected in butchers' shops. It's also been found in unpasteurised milk – yet there is no obligation on manufacturers to say if cheese is made with unpasteurised milk. Despite advice that burgers and other high-risk foods should come with guidelines as to how to cook them correctly, few provide adequate instructions or warnings about the risk of undercooking.

Listeria

Caused by the bacterium *Listeria monocytogenes*, in 1987 listeria hit the headlines with a dramatic increase in the number of reported cases, particularly among pregnant women. It can cause miscarriage, stillbirth or premature labour. In 1989 pregnant women and people with immune system deficiencies were advised not to eat soft ripened cheeses such as brie and camembert, patés, or ready meals unless these were thoroughly reheated. This was a full two years after the Department of Health and MAFF first knew about the risks. Ministers signed 'gagging orders' keeping it secret for two years, during which time 26 babies died.

Today, although the number of cases remains fairly stable, the advice still stands. What makes listeria so worrying is its ability to thrive at temperatures below 5°C – the temperature which we're advised to keep our fridges. In 1996 the Consumers' Association found pre-packed hams containing high levels of bacteria including listeria, suggesting that the use-by dates were too generous or that the hams hadn't been kept cold enough before they were bought.

Salmonella

After a dramatic increase during the 1980s, overall the number of cases of salmonella food poisoning has levelled out somewhat. *Salmonella enteritidis* is by far the most common type; despite attempts to clean up egg and poultry production these foods remain the main source of infection. Avoiding raw or undercooked eggs is the official Government advice.

A new worry is that more resistant types of salmonella bacteria are appearing. For example, 90 per cent of *Salmonella typhimurium*, the second most commonly reported type of salmonella food poisoning, is now resistant to a number of different antibiotics. It's easily spread if animals are stressed or overcrowded; MRM (mechanically recovered meat) can also spread infection.

Campylobacter

Now the most commonly-reported type of food poisoning, with reported cases doubling since the mid-1980s, it has been found that poultry, meat, shellfish and doorstep milk which has been pecked at by birds can all carry the bacteria. It can also be caught from household pets.

KITCHEN HYGIENE

Good kitchen hygiene will help to minimise the risks of food poisoning:

- Wash hands and dry on a clean towel before handling food.
- Keep the fridge clean and make sure it is kept at the correct temperature – below 5°C. The freezer should be kept at minus 18°C.
- Keep raw and cooked foods separate. Thoroughly clean chopping boards to prevent contamination. Raw meat should be stored below cooked foods so that meat juices cannot drip from raw onto cooked foods.
- Defrost meat thoroughly before cooking.
- Make sure all foods are thoroughly cooked, especially if they are cooked in a microwave oven. Poultry, burgers, sausages and mince should be cooked until no pink bits remain.
- Eat leftovers within two days, and don't reheat foods more than once. Never leave food in opened tins.
- Wash all fruit and vegetables thoroughly, especially those that will be eaten raw.

- Follow storage, 'eat by' or 'best before' dates and cooking instructions, particularly for microwave ovens.
- Keep eggs in the fridge and eat before 'best before' dates. Beware of foods such as homemade mayonnaise, mousses and ice cream made with raw eggs.

Ingene-ious Foods

The latest appliance of science to our food is genetic engineering. The UK has been at the forefront of developing new foods using genetically-modified organisms (GMOs), with products already on our supermarket shelves. And that's just the beginning – worldwide over 3,000 genetically-engineered foods are currently being tested. We are promised medicinal bananas, broccoli that can protect against cancer, coffee that is caffeine-free and lower-fat crisps and chips made with potatoes that absorb less fat.

We're told that genetic engineering promises changes to our lives as significant as the development of steam power in the 19th century, or more recently the microchip. So what can we expect? Will gene foods provide us with safer, healthier and more affordable food, as industry promises, or are we all simply unwitting guinea-pigs in a massive experiment for foods whose benefits are still unproven and whose long-term risks are not yet known?

What Is Genetic Engineering?

Genes are the building blocks of living organisms. They are passed from generation to generation and carry the information controlling the hundreds of thousands of characteristics which make up each organism. Now scientists are learning to identify which genes control which characteristics and to transplant genes from one plant or animal to another, altering the genetic material (DNA) of the organism.

Proponents of gene technology argue that it is little more than a speedier version of traditional breeding techniques. But genetic modification can go far beyond what can be achieved by conventional breeding. Genes can now be 'suppressed' – that is, their effects turned off – such as the gene which makes tomatoes lose their firmness quickly. They can also be copied and inserted into another plant or animal, creating new 'transgenic' organisms.

Some of the promised benefits of the genetic engineering of our food include:

- the development of plant crops that have a longer shelf-life, are more resistant to pests, give a higher yield or taste better
- animals which are more resistant to disease, grow faster, are more fertile or produce less fatty meat
- faster food processing
- solutions to world food problems by increasing yields in difficult climates, reducing food losses from pests and diseases, and improving the nutritional value of basic foods.

Guess What's Coming to Dinner?

We've already got cheese made with a genetically-engineered enzyme (*see 'Vegetarian Cheese', page 194*) and tomato paste made from genetically-modified non-squishy FlavrSavr tomatoes (*see 'Non-squishy Tomatoes', page 194*). More controversially, genetically-modified soybeans are now finding their way into literally thousands of foods – up to 60 per cent of processed foods – as well as animal feed (*see 'Spilling the Beans', page 197*). Similarly, a genetically-engineered maize, or corn as it is known in the US, is likely to be used in animal feed and other foods for human consumption. Even more controversially, our daily pinta could in future come courtesy of cows which are regularly injected with the genetically-engineered milk-boosting hormone BST (*see 'BST', page 195*).

In the pipeline are long shelf-life pineapples, slow-ripening bananas and low-caffeine/high-aroma coffee beans. In the animal world, faster growing pigs and even fish (*see 'Supersalmon', page 194*) are being developed. Genes are being transferred between plants and animals, with scientists testing tomatoes containing a fish gene which makes them less prone to damage when frozen and potatoes modified to produce chicken enzymes. Cows with added human genes are being bred to produce human-like milk (*see 'Herman the Bull', page 193*).

Little is free from the scientists' microscopes. Most of the world's important crops, such as wheat, rice, maize, potatoes and soybeans, as well as many vegetable and fruit crops, have been genetically modified; some, including genetically-engineered soya, maize and oilseed rape, are already being grown commercially in the US and Canada.

Herman the Bull

Herman is the world's first transgenic bull with human milk-producing genes. His owners hoped he would be a cow with improved protection against mastitis. In 1993 he sired his first daughters, who are now producing human-style milk. Enormous interest has been shown by the infant formula industry in the potential for developing farm-produced 'mother's milk' for babies.

Supersalmon

Farmed salmon which can grow up to five times the size of normal salmon are being bred in Scotland. The transgenic salmon include a growth hormone gene from another species of fish. By a year old the new fish are five times bigger than their ordinary farmed cousins, and it's claimed they will reach maturity in two rather than three years. The fear is that such salmon may escape and breed with wild salmon and upset the ecological balance.

Vegetarian Cheese

One of the first genetically-modified organisms in food in the UK is the enzyme chymosin, used to make 'vegetarian' cheese since 1992. Cheese made in the traditional way uses rennet from calves' stomachs, which contains chymosin, to coagulate the milk. The demand for rennet now exceeds supply and a number of companies have developed a chymosin produced by genetic modification. The new enzyme is produced by inserting genetic material from calf cells into a yeast which is then grown under controlled conditions.

The resulting chymosin is deemed to be 'nature identical' and there is no legal obligation for cheeses made from it to be labelled. Only the Co-op labels the cheese as a product of genetic engineering. But it's not just 'vegetarian' cheese which may be made from these alternatives to rennets. Much ordinary cheese is also now produced in the same way – so watch out for cheese producers charging premium prices for 'vegetarian' cheese – it can't be justified.

Non-squishy Tomatoes

Tomato paste made from a genetically-engineered tomato was the first genetically-engineered food product to be sold in Europe. Since February 1996 the tomato paste, made with FlavrSavr tomatoes grown in California, has been on sale in Sainsbury's and Safeway.

The FlavrSavr tomato has had its own genes modified to keep it firmer longer. Zeneca, the company which has produced the tomato, claims that the genetic alteration delays the fruit ripening, which results in less waste at harvest, higher yields and increased pectin levels, producing a thicker paste which requires less energy to process. The raw tomatoes cannot be sold in Europe because of the inclusion of an antibiotic marker gene, but its makers Zeneca hope they may be grown in Europe in the future.

BST

Milk conjures up images of purity – the last thing most of us want is our milk being tampered with in any way. Yet that is exactly what has been at stake over the controversial milk-boosting hormone BST.

BST (or bovine somatotropin to give it its full name) is a genetically-engineered growth hormone which is designed to boost milk yields in dairy cows by up to 20 per cent. It has been developed in the US by Monsanto, an agrochemical company which has been pushing to get it approved in Europe.

Consumers don't want it, neither do farmers nor the dairy industry, who don't like the idea of consumers being put off their milk. And we certainly don't need any more milk. The UK Government originally supported its introduction. They were overruled by the European Union, which has banned BST until the end of the century. It has been approved in the US despite the company's own evidence that the hormone can have adverse effects on cows.

The modern dairy cow already produces more milk than nature intended. Regular injections of BST can push cows to produce more milk than their bodies can cope with, reaching a state of metabolic exhaustion which makes them more prone to disease. Soon after its introduction in the US farmers began to report an increase in the number of cows with mastitis (infection of the udder), lameness, inflammation from the repeated injections, and other health problems.

BST first caused a scandal when it was revealed that the controversial hormone was being secretly tested on dairy farms in the UK, with the milk going into the general milk supply. Although its use on farms may be banned in Europe there's nothing to stop dairy products, like mozzarella cheese made from BST-produced milk in the US, from being imported and legally sold in the UK. And there's nothing on the label to tell you.

PESTS AND DISEASES

As modern agriculture has intensified so the problems of pests and diseases have grown. Now genetic engineering is hoping to solve some of these problems by developing insect- and virus-resistant varieties of common crops, from cucumbers, corn and potatoes to strawberries.

First to hit the market and the headlines is a US-grown maize which has been genetically engineered to produce a natural toxin lethal to many caterpillars and grubs, including the European corn borer, the scourge of conventionally grown maize. This is achieved by inserting genes from soil bacteria known as *Bacillus thuringiensis* (or *Bt* for short) which naturally produce the toxin. *Bt* toxins are widely used in organic farming as an environmentally benign insecticide.

The promise is that the genetically-engineered crops will be sprayed with less insecticides, but there's a downside too. Ecologists believe that *Bt* maize will expose insects to massive doses of the natural toxin and will accelerate the development of *Bt*-resistant pests. Not only could that spell the end for the effectiveness of *Bt* toxin as an environmentally safe method of pest control as used by organic farmers, it could mean that maize growers have to revert to even higher doses of toxic chemicals to control pests.

Despite these concerns the import of *Bt* maize has been given the go-ahead by the European Union and is likely to be mainly used in animal feed but could also be used in foods such as breakfast cereals and snacks, without any labelling. Yet Government advisers have raised safety fears about antibiotic marker genes in unprocessed maize being fed to farm animals. There are fears that such marker genes could spread anti-biotic resistance to farm animals, making bacterial infections harder to treat (*see*

'Are Gene Foods Safe?', page 199). Major supermarket chains share these concerns and say they will not sell meat or eggs from animals fed the gene-altered maize.

And if that weren't enough, *Bt* maize also contains a gene to make it resistant to the weedkiller glufosinate. In the chemical battle against weeds it's just one of a number of new strains of 'herbicide-resistant' crops genetically engineered to be resistant to common weedkillers. Herbicides can now be sprayed onto the gene-altered crops, killing the weeds but leaving the crops undamaged.

Splicing genes to produce herbicide-resistance is the most prevalent use of genetic engineering. More than half of all the gene-altered crops being tested in the EU are herbicide-resistant. Despite the industry's PR gloss that genetic engineering will bring benefits for consumers, such crops offer no real benefits to consumers – yet do pose possible environmental risks, including:

- **possible increased use of chemical herbicides**
- **risk of herbicide-resistant genes spreading to other plants** – producing 'superweeds' which are even harder to control
- **new crops that could become weeds themselves** – affecting wild flora and wildlife.

Such risks mean that the utmost care should be taken in the development, introduction and use of genetically-engineered crops. Yet many critics do not consider this to be happening. As Sir Crispin Tickell, Chair of the British Government Panel on Sustainable Development, said in 1996: 'Monitoring seems to be conspicuously lacking in what happens. We don't know what happens to these genetically-modified organisms over a period of time.'

Spilling the Beans

The humble soybean has taken centre stage in a global controversy over the safety and ethics of genetic engineering and the right of consumers to know what is in the food they eat.

In November 1996 the first genetically-engineered soybeans to arrive in Europe from the US were greeted with a storm of protest. At the heart of the protests – made by food and environmental campaigners as well as supermarkets and health food manufacturers – is anger that genetically-modified soya will not be kept separate or labelled.

The new soybean, developed by Monsanto, a US multinational chemical company, has been genetically modified with genes from a bacteria, a virus and a petunia to make it resistant to the company's top-selling weedkiller, Roundup. Critics say it's just a new use for an old chemical. Certainly it's of clear financial benefit to the company, which can now sell a package of soybeans and the chemical to farmers. But it's not of such benefit to the environment, as it will mean more chemical sprayings, nor to consumers, though they will have little choice over whether to eat it or not.

Soya and soya oil are used in over 7,000 common food products. So it will be hard to avoid the new beans. UK food manufacturers, represented by the Food and Drink Federation (FDF), say separating the genetically-engineered variety from traditionally grown ones would be 'impracticable', 'unnecessary' and 'unenforceable'. The first new soybeans harvested in the US were mixed with conventional soybeans for export to Europe. The FDF says consumers can choose by avoiding all products containing soya. But this may not always be easy or practical, particularly for vegetarians.

The beans were cleared for sale in Europe, following proposals from the UK Government to allow its importation. But while there is no evidence of harmful health effects from the modified soya at present, no safety tests on the effects on humans of eating the new soya have ever been carried out.

Reading the Label

It's hard to avoid soya. An estimated 60 per cent of the processed food we eat contains soya in one form or another: as an oil, flour, vegetable protein or as an emulsifier. It's found in everything from bread, chocolate, cakes and margarine to ice cream and pasta, and is the basis of many vegetarian foods.

Food manufacturers say if consumers want to avoid genetically-engineered soya they will have to avoid all soya-containing foods. That means reading the small print of ingredient lists – but even this may not be enough. Soya finds its way into foods in forms which may not be easy to decipher in the labelling, as in vegetable proteins, vegetable oils and lecithin (see 'Hidden Soya Ingredients, page 13).

Are Gene Foods Safe?

Of course the $64 million question about gene foods is – are they safe? Unfortunately there is no simple answer. Genetic engineering is such a new science that there is still much that scientists don't know. Although gene modifications may seem harmless, their effects can be hard to predict. This is why consumer and environmental organisations are arguing that it is important to be cautious. After all, BSE has taught us that what may look like simple changes in food production can have devastating effects in years to come.

Although its proponents liken genetic engineering to the selection of characteristics by traditional breeding methods, genetic engineering is not subject to the same intricate limiting mechanisms and so cannot be compared to natural selection processes. Genetic engineering leads to genetic combinations that in many cases would never occur in nature, opening up new metabolic pathways with consequences which may not come to light for some time. This makes it impossible to say that we know that all genetically-engineered foods are completely without risk – or similarly that all might be dangerous.

Whatever your moral or ethical stance on genetically-engineered foods, what is important, from a safety point of view, is that each new food or food made using genetically-modified organisms is assessed individually. Some products may offer genuine benefits and be safe, while others could pose some kind of hazard. Until we know more we should proceed slowly, making

sure that there are adequate safeguards in place and that consumers have as much information as possible.

Some of the potential problems that are already recognised include:

Natural Toxins

In one early experiment, scientists developed a genetically-modified strain of potato that was more resistant to crop damage. But
they also found that the levels of the potato's natural toxin,
solanin, increased to such a level that the potatoes were poisonous to eat.

Allergies

Another concern is the risk of allergies. There are fears that
transgenic plants engineered for resistance to disease and pests
may be more likely to cause allergies than unmodified plants. In
the US soybeans genetically modified to include genes from a
Brazil nut caused allergy in susceptible people. The product was
voluntarily withdrawn from the market. Other problems of this
kind may not be so easy to identify.

Antibiotic Resistance

Another concern is that some GMOs may increase the risk of an-
tibiotic-resistance in humans and farm animals. In genetic engineering, genes which confer resistance to an antibiotic are often
used as 'marker genes'. Such marker genes are attached to the
gene that the scientist wants to transfer to indicate whether the
gene transfer has been successful. In the presence of an antibiotic the plants with the new characteristic will grow, making them
easy to distinguish from those for which gene transfer was not
successful. The concern is that antibiotic resistance could spread
to bacteria in our bodies, or in farm animals, making us (and/or
them) resistant to antibiotics and making bacterial infections
harder to treat.

Virtually all genetically-engineered crops developed in the
US use antibiotic marker genes. Cooking destroys the antibiotic

resistance, however, which is why the UK Government has only approved the sale in the UK of the cooked FlavrSavr tomato paste, and not the raw tomatoes. But at the end of 1996 the Government protested that it had no powers to stop genetically-modified corn (maize) which carries an antibiotic marker from being imported into Europe. As there were plans for the maize to be used raw in animal feed, experts warned the Government that there was a risk of resistance to the antibiotic ampicillin, spreading to farm animals and even possibly to humans. There are alternatives to antibiotic markers but the industry says they would be more costly to use.

Environmental Effects

We also don't know enough about the effects of growing genetically-modified crops on the environment and the ecological balance of nature. If crops like soya or maize which are genetically-modified to be resistant to pests or weedkillers breed with their wild relatives, there are fears that resistant 'superweeds' could be created which could not be controlled by conventional weedkillers. In addition, modified genes could also recombine with bacteria or viruses, creating new and wholly unknown strains that may be hazardous.

Insects and other pests are very adept at evolving to changing circumstances. Thus we've come to see bacteria that are resistant to antibiotics and pests that are resistant to chemical pesticides. It is probably only a matter of time before pests would evolve to become resistant to gene modifications built into crops, creating new and possibly deadlier superbugs.

SAFETY FIRST?

We quite rightly expect that new foods, ingredients or additives are tested for safety before they can go on sale. Campaigners are worried that the approval assessments for most genetically-engineered foods will be little more than a notification procedure. In addition, the rules, as laid down in the EC's 'Novel Food

Regulations', will not cover many genetically-engineered processing aids such as enzymes and additives, and will not require any monitoring of the effects of gene foods in the population when they become more widely consumed.

In the UK the Ministry of Agriculture's Advisory Committee on Novel Foods and Processes (ACNFP) operates an entirely voluntary approval process. So far all new gene foods on sale have been approved by the ACNFP, but the Committee does not take into account the 'need' for a novel food or ingredient – something that the manufacturers of additives must prove. This discrepancy between the two approval processes raises the question of why additives, which might be consumed in minute quantities, are submitted to more stringent safeguards than novel foods, which could be consumed in far greater quantities.

The UK authorities have not yet allowed any genetically-engineered crops to be grown by British farmers, though they have approved the sale of a number of gene foods products. Under global trade agreements individual countries have little or no power to stop the import of foods grown and produced elsewhere in the world. As there are no internationally agreed safety standards for genetically-engineered foods, we are already eating foods made from ingredients which cannot be produced here but which are allowed in another country and imported into the UK.

Apart from the case of genetically-engineered soya, already described, there is that of dairy products made from milk produced using the genetically-engineered growth hormone BST. While BST is banned in Europe it is permitted in the US, and dairy products such as cheese possibly made from BST milk are quite legally sold in Europe and unwittingly eaten by consumers.

We need to see internationally agreed safety standards to ensure that, no matter how small the risks, consumer safety should come first.

The Right to Know What You Are Eating

There will be no way of knowing whether you are eating most genetically-engineered foods. They will look, smell and taste the same as foods produced conventionally. The only way you will know is if they are labelled. Yet only organic foods can be guaranteed to be free of genetically-modified ingredients.

Despite consumers' desire to have more information about the food they are eating and to know whether genetically-modified ingredients have been used, they will largely be kept in the dark. Some manufacturers fear that labelling will blunt consumers' appetite for gene foods, although where products have been labelled (such as the Co-op's vegetarian cheese) and where there are no over-riding safety concerns, there is no evidence that consumers are not buying the product.

TO LABEL OR NOT TO LABEL

For the vast majority of foods made with genetically-modified ingredients there will be no legal obligation on manufacturers to label their products (e.g. sugar from genetically-engineered sugar beet, oil and lecithin from genetically-altered soya, tomato ketchup made with long-life tomatoes). Only in a few circumstances will a declaration be required: specifically, if a food made from genetically-altered ingredients:

- contains living genetically-modified organisms
- contains material which might affect health (as in the case of people with allergies)
- could meet with ethical objections (such as human genes in foods, animals in plant foods for vegetarians or animal genes which are the subject of religious or dietary requirements, for example from a pig or a cow)
- is nutritionally different from conventional foods.

This flies in the face of one of the most basic consumer rights – the right to know what we are buying. Why should we be denied information on gene foods?

Some companies have decided voluntarily to declare information. The tomato paste made from gene modified FlavrSavr tomatoes, sold by Sainsbury's and Safeway, is labelled with the words 'made with genetically-modified tomatoes' while the Co-op's vegetarian cheeses made with genetically-altered chymosin declares that it is 'produced using gene technology'.

But there is no requirement for the hundreds and thousands of foods that might contain the new genetically-engineered soya to be labelled. Protests by consumer and environmental organisations have been augmented by supermarkets and health food manufacturers who want to avoid the use of genetically-modified soya in their own products.

But what should be written on labels? When genetically-engineered crops such as soya are mixed with a conventionally produced harvest, then even the manufacturers and retailers simply won't know which type of soya they have been using. Declaring that all soya-containing foods 'may contain genetically-engineered soya' is unclear and unhelpful. The only way manufacturers and retailers could give consumers a real choice would be for genetically-engineered soya to be segregated at source, but that's been ruled as impossible by US soya producers. However, EC legislation will now allow manufacturers to tell consumers if foods are *not* the product of genetic engineering, enabling those producers who can, for example, guarantee a supply of non-modified soya to declare that their product does not contain genetically-engineered soya.

Missing information

Leading supermarkets are in breach of their own industry's guidelines on labelling genetically-modified (GM) foods, according to the Consumers' Association. Following concern among consumers about foods containing GM ingredients such as soya, the supermarkets agreed to provide information for shoppers about GM ingredients and the foods which may contain them. Voluntary guidelines were agreed by the Institute of Grocery Distribution, of which all the major supermarket chains are members. But in mid-1997 the Consumers' Association found major stores failing to provide such information to the public.

Gene Baby Foods

There are no restrictions on the use of genetically-altered food ingredients in baby foods and baby milks unless products are sold as organic. It is unlikely that most non-organic baby food manufacturers will be able to guarantee that their products are free of genetically-engineered ingredients once their current supplies of non-modified ingredients have run out.

The Ethical Dimension

'At the moment, as is so often the case with technology, we seem to spend most of our time establishing what is technically possible, and then a little time trying to establish whether or not it is likely to be safe, without ever stopping to ask whether it is something we should be doing in the first place.' So spoke Prince Charles at the Lady Eve Balfour Memorial Lecture in 1996, echoing the concerns that many feel about the new ethical questions that genetic engineering poses.

Genetic manipulation raises ethical concerns about the right of scientists to 'play God' with living organisms. Genetic engineering for medical purposes may help to save lives, but tinkering with genes for food opens up a whole new set of questions – for example, is it cannibalism to eat foods into which human genes have been inserted? It's a question that arose over sheep into which human genes were incorporated to produce medically valuable human proteins in their milk. Such was the extent of failed experiments that the Department of Health was asked to rule whether such animals could be used for food. The Government's ethical advisors, the Polkinghorne Committee, recommended that eating animals from failed experiments was OK, provided they had not been genetically modified in any way.

Similarly, those with religious dietary laws may not wish to eat food to which genes from animals whose flesh is forbidden has been transferred. Already in the US cattle have been modified to carry the porcine growth hormone from pigs. Similarly, vegetarians may be unhappy about vegetables with genes from animals. And should we be concerned about the use, as animal feed, of organisms containing human genes? These are not easy questions to answer. But while scientists may be able to supply 'rational' answers as to why these practices may be acceptable, for many people it will remain a matter of personal values and beliefs.

There is also the question of animal welfare and any suffering that genetically-engineered farm animals may experience. In experiments, so-called 'self-shearing' sheep injected with genetically-engineered hormones suffered increased abortion rates, genetically-engineered chickens with supposed greater resistance to salmonella died from cancer, and some genetically-engineered pigs and sheep have damaged joints, diabetes-like symptoms, impaired vision and shorter lives.[1] The 'Beltsville pigs' in the US were given human growth hormone genes to accelerate growth, only to suffer from arthritis, stomach ulcers, lethargy and impotence. And the rush to push farm animals beyond their natural limits may place unacceptable stresses on livestock (see 'BST', page 195).

Dolly the Sheep

The world was shocked when in February 1997 the news of Dolly the Sheep, the first clone of an adult animal ever to be created, hit the headlines. Yet this landmark in biological research has raised alarms that such techniques could be used to create human clones.

Dolly was developed from an udder cell by a team of British scientists at the Roslin Institute in Edinburgh. She is genetically identical to the sheep from which the cell was taken. Less well publicised are the failures of cloning experimentation on animals. Problems with animals failing to survive in the womb, being abnormally large at birth or being malformed are commonplace. Other reports include calves with genetic material from chickens whose muscles turn jelly-like at 15 weeks. Animal welfare campaigners say this suffering and surgical intervention, which is of no benefit to the animal, is unethical, and that experiments should be stopped.

The Roslin scientists have predicted that in 20 years' time 85 per cent of British cattle could be clones. Yet it's hard to see what practical benefits this would bring. Genetically-identical animals would also be identically susceptible to disease. If one animal became infected, the disease could sweep like wildfire through the rest of the herd, putting farmers' livelihoods at risk.

Pharming?

'Pharming' is the newest and potentially most lucrative biotechnology development. It involves producing medicinal products from genetically-engineered plants and animals. Sheep are already producing milk containing a protein used to treat the lung disease emphysema, and goats are producing milk with a human antibody useful in cancer therapy. Even more revolutionary are likely to be edible vaccines to confer immunity to disease. Scientists are already experimenting with bananas to deliver a vaccine against cholera and diarrhoea. It could be a cheaper alternative to traditional vaccines and would eliminate the need for storage at low temperatures, as bananas do not require refrigeration. And the bananas could always be re-engineered to prevent them rotting!

FEAST OR FAMINE

Whenever there is a debate on genetic engineering you are likely to hear its proponents say that the technology should be encouraged because it is going to feed the world's hungry people. If this were true then such an objective would demand support, but in reality there's little evidence to give credence to the claim.

First, most research is focusing not on staple crops on which subsistence farmers and many of the world's poor depend, but upon more profitable crops to be grown in the developed world. Secondly, higher costs mean genetically-engineered crops are beyond the means of poorer farmers. Seeds for such crops are more expensive to buy, and the crops themselves tend to need expensive applications of chemicals. In general 'peasant farming' is far more efficient in that it uses less of the world's resources than 'agrochemical' farming. In the long run, small-scale farming will feed the world best.

And, far from being the latest 'quick-fix' solution to world hunger, there's evidence that genetic engineering may actually damage the trade prospects of developing countries. It's possible that crops which can now only be grown in warmer parts of the world could be engineered so they could grow in colder climates. And the use of genetic engineering to produce substitutes for raw materials such as sugar, coffee, palm oil and cocoa butter could devastate the economies of many poor countries.

The Future

Whatever your views on genetically-modified foods, there is one area where there seems to be general agreement on all sides – the need for more information and open debate. Biotechnology companies are beginning to recognise that there are no short-cuts to winning consumer confidence; it is inevitable that confidence will only be gained through a process of involvement, consultation and acceptance of consumer opinion. They may even have to accept the unpalatable truth – that while some products may be accepted, others will be rejected.

Taking Action

Many people first want to know more about what's in their food because they are worried. Anxieties about BSE, food poisoning, additives, pesticide residues or what genetic engineering might bring exist alongside the worries of whether we are eating healthily or are giving our children a good start in life. And it's easy to feel angry, too – angry about the lack of information we are given, angry about the way decisions have been made and angry that the loopholes in the law mean clever companies can pull the wool over our eyes about the true nature of their products.

But it's a pity if such anxieties and anger take the pleasure out of food and eating. Turning anxiety and anger into action means we can put pressure on companies to produce better food and we can make sure our voices can be heard when it comes to official decision-making.

How to Take Action

Get Informed

Reading this book is a great start to knowing more about what's in your food and how to make safer and healthier food choices. Many of the organisations listed in this chapter can provide further information on particular issues such as genetic engineering, animal welfare and sustainable food production, or on health concerns such as allergies, hyperactivity and eating disorders. Organisations such as the Consumers' Association publish product surveys, food policy information and advice in its *Which?* and *Which? Health* magazines. The *Food Magazine* (published quarterly by the Food Commission) provides a regular update on food campaigns and investigations.

Support Producers of Better Quality Products

Buying organic food, truly animal welfare-friendly meat and eggs, fair-traded foods or locally grown produce sends a clear message to producers and to retailers. It's only through increased demand for these products that they will be more widely available. They may cost slightly more but at least you know the extra cost is helping to support farming that is kinder to the environment and to animals, and safer for the people who are producing it and for the people who are eating it. There's the added benefit that it might taste better, too.

Let Them Know

If you think your supermarket could be doing better, for example by stocking more organic produce or making sure that they label foods containing genetically-modified ingredients – let them know. You can speak to the manager of your local store, but it's also worth writing to the head office (*see addresses below*). Supermarkets are so competitive now that they are extremely sensitive to consumers' views – they don't want to lose your custom. Changes might not happen overnight but your letter *will* have an impact.

Write to the Manufacturer

If you have a query about a particular product, contact the manufacturer – their name and address should be on the packaging. If it's something more serious, for example food that contains foreign bodies, causes food poisoning or appears to be incorrectly or misleadingly labelled, then also contact your local environmental health or trading standards department at your Town Hall (*see below*).

Support Campaigning Organisations

Organisations that campaign for safer, healthier food – many are listed at the end of this chapter – are largely funded by the support of individuals like yourself. Your subscription or donation can help to ensure that an organisation will be in a position to take your concerns to the highest level.

Let Your MP and MEP Know

Never before has food been such a political issue. And with plans for a new food agency to improve food safety and decision-making, now is the time to let politicians know your views and to ensure their promises are kept. For too long food companies have been able to bend the ear of politicians behind closed doors. It's now time for a truly independent food agency in which consumers get a fair hearing.

How to Complain

As a nation we don't like to complain too much. When we're asked in a restaurant if we're enjoying our meal we're much more likely to say meekly, 'Oh yes, thank you' than 'the waiter was rude, we waited an hour for our meal and then when it arrived it was cold.' We just don't want to be seen to be 'making a fuss'. But any good business will welcome comments, including criticisms. It's only by getting feedback from their customers that they can make improvements and rectify what went wrong.

We have a right by law to expect that food shall be 'of the nature, substance and quality demanded' – note the word *demanded*. So if you discover that what you've bought doesn't live up to your expectations then you've a right to take it back to the shop where you bought it. They are responsible for the food they sell and should be able to sort out the problem. In the battle for your custom, supermarkets have become extremely sensitive to customer complaints and concerns, and some now offer a no-quibbles money-back guarantee. Really this should apply to all food businesses.

By law food must also be of satisfactory quality and be safe, but who do you turn to when something is seriously wrong? **Trading Standards Officers and Environmental Health Officers** work on behalf of the public to ensure that foods are safe and correctly labelled.

In general environmental health officers are responsible for food safety and hygiene. They check food businesses, including shops, manufacturers and restaurants, to ensure that hygiene standards and practices are up to scratch. If necessary they can ask for improvements to be made and even close down premises. In cases of food poisoning they can investigate to try and find the source of the bug, particularly if it has affected a number of people. If you buy food which is contaminated take it to your local Environmental Health Department.

As far as food is concerned, Trading Standards Officers (the old Weights and Measures Inspectors) are generally more concerned with matters relating to how food is sold, checking that the public are not being short changed. For example they can check food labelling to try and decide whether products really are what they claim to be.

Each local authority will organise its consumer services differently; some have two separate departments while others have combined the two under a Consumer Protection Department. You can contact them via your local Town Hall. Consumer Protection Departments generally also offer advice and information.

Both environmental health and trading standards officers have the powers to take companies to court if it's considered they have broken the law, though this is not always easy. In some cases, such as misleading labelling, the law is not always clear-cut – which makes it difficult for food law enforcement officers to bring a case to court. In others, companies can get off the hook by claiming 'due diligence'; that is, even though they did, for example, sell food that was unsafe or described incorrectly, they had taken adequate precautions to try and prevent this happening.

If you buy contaminated food you may be able to get compensation from the retailer or from the manufacturer. You have to have been injured if you want to make a legal claim against them, although some may offer some form of compensation as a gesture of goodwill even if no injury has been incurred.

HOW TO COMPLAIN ABOUT ADVERTISING

There are separate regulatory bodies depending on the media in which adverts appear (*see below*). These are responsible for investigating complaints about inaccurate or misleading claims in advertising or matters of taste and decency.

Many people may feel they lack the expertise to submit a complaint, but you don't need to be an 'expert' to let the regulatory bodies know your views. Each regulatory body publishes a 'code of practice' which lays down the rules and principles to which advertising must adhere.

You know if you've been offended by an advert, but it can be harder to tell if you've been misled. But if you think that an advert is misleading or inaccurate, then the chances are others do too. If in doubt, complain.

Advertising must be 'legal, decent, honest and truthful' and it should not mislead – either by what it says or by what it fails to say. Advertisers should be able to provide scientific evidence to support any health or nutrition claims that they make, though this hasn't stopped some from going over the top. It's more likely in newspaper and magazine adverts because these are not approved in advance, unlike TV adverts which must be cleared before transmission. Inaccurate or misleading advertising can easily cause confusion and undermine our ability to make healthier food choices.

There are special rules covering advertising and children which are supposed to take into account children's immaturity and natural credulity. However, the amount of food advertising to children for unhealthy fatty and sugary foods has raised concerns. For more information on this and how to complain about food advertising in general, contact the National Food Alliance (*address below*).

The Independent Television Commission (ITC)
  33 Foley Street
  London W1P 7LB
  Tel: 0171 255 3000
Regulates all television advertising and commercial sponsorship including that on satellite and cable TV channels which are based in the UK.

The Advertising Standards Authority (ASA)
  2 Torrington Place
  London WC1E 8HF
  Tel: 0171 580 5555
Responsible for all printed and non-broadcast advertising including adverts (and 'advertorials') in magazines and newspapers, poster advertising, cinema commercials as well as promotional leaflets and other marketing literature.

Radio Authority
  Holbrook House
  14 Great Queen Street
  London WC2B 5DG
  Tel: 0171 430 2724
Regulates advertising and sponsorship on commercial radio.

Supermarkets

You can contact the supermarkets' head offices (write to Customer Services) at the following addresses:

ASDA
  ASDA House
  South Bank
  Great Wilson Street
  Leeds LS11 5AD

Co-op
  CWS
  PO Box 53
  New Century House
  Manchester M60 4ES

Marks & Spencer
  St Michael House
  47 Baker Street
  London W1A 1DN

Safeway
  Beddow Way
  Aylesford
  Maidstone
  Kent ME20 7AT

J Sainsbury
  Stamford House
  Stamford Street
  London SE1 9LS

Somerfield
  Somerfield House
  Whitchurch Lane
  Bristol BS14 OJT

Tesco
Tesco House
Delamare Road
Cheshunt
Herts EN8 9SL

Waitrose
Doncastle Road
Southern Industrial Area
Bracknell
Berks RG12 8YA

Where to Go for Further Help and Information

The Ministry of Agriculture, Fisheries and Food (MAFF) has two helplines:

- **MAFF Helpline**: 0645 335 577 (local rate) can provide information about agriculture and fisheries, including information on BSE and food labelling.
- **The Food Safety and Legislation Helpline**: 0345 573 012 (local rate) can provide information and advice about food laws and safety.

In addition, **Foodline**: 0800 282 407 (freephone), which is sponsored by the major supermarkets, provides information on food safety.

ORGANISATIONS

Always include a SAE with any letters you send to these organisations – many work with limited resources.

Action and Information on Sugars
PO Box 459
London SE5 7QA

Baby Milk Action
23 St Andrews Street
Cambridge CB2 3AX

British Heart Foundation
14 Fitzharding Street
London W1X 4DH

Caroline Walker Trust
12 Thistle Grove
London SW10 9RZ

Compassion in World Farming
Charles House
5a Charles Street
Petersfield GU32 3EH

Consumers' Association
2 Marylebone Road
London NW1 4DF

Elm Farm Research Centre
Hamstead Marshall
Nr Newbury
Berks RG15 0HR

Ethical Consumer
ECRA Publishing Ltd
5th floor
16 Nicholas Street
Manchester M1 4EJ

Fairtrade Foundation
Regent House
89 Kingsway
London WC2B 6RH

The Food Commission
3rd floor
5–11 Worship Street
London EC2A 2BH

Food for Health Network
PO Box 972
London EC2A 2JE

Friends of the Earth
26 Underwood Street
London N1 7JT

Genetics Forum
3rd floor
5–11 Worship Street
London EC2A 2BH

Greenpeace
Canonbury Villas
London N1 2PM

Health Education Authority
Hamilton House
Mabledon Place
London WC1H 9TX

National Consumer Council
20 Grosvenor Gardens
London SW1W 0DH

National Federation of Consumer Groups
  48 Kingswood Road
  Shortlands
  Bromley BR2 0NF

National Food Alliance
  5–11 Worship Street
  London EC2A 2BH

National Heart Forum
  Tavistock House
  Tavistock Square
  London WC1H 9LG

New Consumer
  52 Elswick Road
  Newcastle upon Tyne NE4 5BR

Northern Ireland Chest, Heart & Stroke Association
  21 Dublin Road
  Belfast BT2 7FS

Organic Food and Farming Centre/Soil Association
  86 Colston Street
  Bristol BS1 5BB

OXFAM
  Banbury Road
  Oxford OX2 7DX

Pesticides Trust
  Eurolink Business Centre
  49 Effra Road
  London SW2 1BZ

Royal Society for the Prevention of Cruelty to Animals (RSPCA)
Causeway
Horsham
West Sussex RH12 1HG

School Meals Campaign
PO Box 402
London WC1H 9TZ

Sustainable Agriculture, Food and Environment (SAFE) Alliance
36 Ebury Street
London SW1W 0LU
Tel: 0171 823 5660

Vegan Society
33–35 George Street
Oxford OX1 2AY

Vegetarian Society
Parkdale
Dunham Road
Altrincham
Cheshire WA14 4OJ

Women's Environmental Network
87 Worship Street
London EC2A 2BE

World Cancer Research Fund
105 Park Street
London W1Y 3FB

SELF-HELP AND SUPPORT GROUPS

Action Against Allergy
  PO Box 278
  Twickenham TW1 4QQ

The Anaphylaxis Campaign
(for peanut and other nut allergies)
  8 Wey Close
  Ash
  Aldershot
  Hampshire GU12 6LY

British Diabetic Association
  10 Queen Anne Street
  London W1M 0BD

Coeliac Society
  PO Box 220
  High Wycombe
  Bucks HP11 2HY

Dietbreakers
  Barford St Michael
  Banbury OX15 0UA

Eating Disorders Association
  1st floor, Wensun House
  103 Prince of Wales Road
  Norwich NR1 1DW

Family Heart Association
  Wesley House
  7 High Street
  Kidlington
  Oxford OX5 2DH

Foresight
(Association for Pre-conceptual Care)
   28 The Paddock
   Godalming
   Surrey GU7 1XD

Hyperactive Children's Support Group
   71 Whyke Lane
   Chichester
   West Sussex PO19 2LD

National Association for Colitis and Crohn's Disease
   98a London Road
   St Albans
   Herts AL1 1NX

National Asthma Campaign
   Providence House
   Providence Place
   London N1 0NT

National Eczema Society
   Tavistock House North
   Tavistock Square
   London WC1H 9SR

National Osteoporosis Society
   Barton Meade House
   PO Box 10
   Radstock
   Bath BA3 3YB

Pesticides Exposure Group of Sufferers (PEGS)
   4 Lloyd House
   Regent Terrace
   Cambridge CB2 1AA

Women's Nutritional Advisory Service
   PO Box 268
   Lewes
   East Sussex BN7 2QN

TRADE ASSOCIATIONS

The Food and Drink Federation
   6 Catherine Street
   London WC2B 5JJ
Main trade association representing UK food manufacturers.

British Retail Consortium
   5 Grafton Street
   London W1X 3LB

National Farmers Union
   Agriculture House
   164 Shaftesbury Avenue
   London WC2H 8HL

Reference Notes

Chapter 1

1. *Which?* April 1996, Consumers' Association.
2. Food Commission, *Food Magazine* 23, November 1993.
3. *Which?* June 1997, Consumers' Association.
4. Southwark's Public Protection Dept, *Food Magazine* 5, 1989.
5. Food Commission, *Food Magazine* 32, January 1996.
6. Ministry of Agriculture, Fisheries and Food, *Food Chemical Surveillance Annual Report*, 1996.
7. *Health Which?* October 1996, Consumers' Association.
8. *Which?* April 1996, Consumers' Association.
9. Food Commission, *Food Magazine* 23, November 1993.

Chapter 2

1. *Health Which?* October 1996, Consumers' Association.
2. 'Artificial sweetener "Sunett" should not be used in diet soda, new tests needed, cancer experts tell FDA', news

release, Center for Science in the Public Interest, Washington DC, July 31st, 1996.

3. H. J. Roberts, 'Aspartame and headaches', *Neurology* 45.8, 1995: page 1631.
4. E. Millstone, 'Sweet and sour: the unanswered questions about Aspartame', *Ecologist* 24.2, March/April 1994.
5. J. W. Olney *et al.*, 'Increasing brain tumour rates: Is there a link to aspartame?', *Neuropathology and Experimental Neurology* 55, 11th November 1996.

Chapter 3

1. *Which?* August 1995, Consumers' Association.
2. Food Commission, 'Low-fat foods', *The Food Magazine* 27, October 1994.
3. Action and Information on Sugars, *Sugar Claims: Straight and Credible, Slippery and Cunning*, 1997.
4. Law *et al.*, *British Medical Journal*, 302, 1991.
5. Nutritional Aspects of Cardiovascular Disease, COMA Cardiovascular Review Group, Department of Health, HMSO, 1994.
6. *British Medical Journal* 312, 18th May 1996: page 1239.
7. Research Services Ltd, 'Nutrition Labelling Study Report', MAFF, 1995.
8. National Consumer Council, *Messages on Food*, 1997.
9. 'Functional Foods Examined', Food Commission, 1996.
10. Food Commission, *Food Magazine* 38, 1997.
11. *Which?* March 1997, Consumers' Association.
12. 'Preventing coronary heart disease. The role of antioxidants, vegetables and fruit', National Heart Forum, 1997.

Chapter 4

1. 'Children's Food', Mintel, August 1996.
2. Flora Project for Heart Disease Prevention, in collaboration with *She* magazine, 1994.
3. 'A spoonful of sugar', Consumers International, November 1996.
4. National Consumer Council, 'Sponsorship in Schools', 1996.
5. 'A spoonful of sugar', Consumers International, November 1996.
6. Summary of the Judgement, McDonald's Corporation and McDonald's Restaurants Ltd against Helen Marie Steel and David Morris, Case No 1990-M-No.5724, High Court of Justice Queen's Bench Division, 19 June 1997.
7. *Web of Deception: Threats to Children from Online Marketing*, Center for Media Education, Washington DC, 1996.
8. Food Commission, 'Snack Attack', *Food Magazine* 21, 1993.
9. Nathan *et al.*, *British Journal of Nutrition* 75, 1996: pages 533–44.
10. Food Commission, *Food Magazine* 31, 1995.
11. *Cracking the Code*, Interagency Group of Breastfeeding Monitoring, 1997.
12. Food Commission, *Food Magazine* 37, 1997.
13. COMA Report on Weaning and the Weaning Diet, Department of Health, 1994.
14. Food Commission, *Food Magazine* 37, 1997.
15. Rolles, J. *et al.*, *Archives of Diseases of Childhood* 1995: pages 137–40.

Chapter 5

1. Department of Health, 'Obesity: Reversing the increasing problem of obesity in England', Nutrition and Physical Activity Task Force, HMSO, 1995.

2. see Sanders, T., Bazalgette, P., *You Don't Have to Diet*, Bantam, 1994.
3. Garrow, J. S., 'Obesity and Overweight', Health Education Authority, 1991.
4. Please note: people who are clinically obese need medical advice.
5. Hill. A. J., 'Pre-adolescent dieting', *International Review of Psychiatry* 5, 1993: pages 87–100.
6. The Food Commission, 'The Slimming Scandal', *Food Magazine* 16, 1992.
7. Coronary Prevention Group, 'Lean Pickings', *Food Magazine* 17, 1992.
8. White Paper on Olestra, Center for Science in the Public Interest, Washington DC, 1996.
9. *Slim Hopes*, National Food Alliance, 1996.

Chapter 6

1. 'Preventing coronary heart disease. The role of antioxidants, vegetables and fruit', National Heart Forum, 1997.
2. Food Adulteration, London Food Commission, 1988.
3. *Pesticides News* 33, Pesticides Trust, September 1996.
4. Food Quality: Concepts and Methodology, Elm Farm Research Centre, 1992.

Chapter 7

1. *Which? Way to Health*, February 1995, Consumers' Association.
2. *Which?* March 1997, Consumers' Association.
3. Ibid.
4. Veterinary Medicines Directorate's surveillance scheme January–December 1994.
5. *Health Which?* June 1996, Consumers' Association.

6. *Which?* January 1996, Consumers' Association.
7. *Which?* October 1996, Consumers' Association.
8. *Which?* September 1995, Consumers' Association.
9. Food Commission, *Food Magazine* 37, April 1997.

Chapter 8

1. 'Gene Transfer and the Welfare of Farm Animals', Compassion in World Farming, 1995.

Index

Abattoirs 168, 181, 187
Acceptable Daily Intake (ADI) 145
ACE vitamins *see* Vitamins and
  minerals
Acesulfame-K 45, 50, 68, 128
Action and Information on Sugars
  (AIS) 65
Additives 5, 7, 9, 12, 16, 29, 31,
  35–53, 99, 100, 101–2, 114–15,
  117, 129
 allergies 41
 antioxidants 39, 45
 approval of 41
 artificial sweeteners 20, 39, 45,
  49–52, 68, 99, 102, 114–15,
  127–8
 babies and young children 46,
  49, 99, 101, 114
 in bottled water 16
 bulk sweeteners 45, 50, 52

colourings 14, 16, 18, 20, 22–3,
  39, 42, 43, 44, 46–7, 48, 49, 99,
  101, 117, 164, 170, 173
 cosmetic 41
 emulsifiers 39, 41, 43, 45
 flavourings 5, 7, 20, 39, 42, 45,
  99, 101, 102
 mineral hydrocarbon oils and
  waxes 47
 natural/nature-identical 22–3, 48
 polyphosphates 29, 43
 preservatives 39, 40, 43, 44–5, 49
 processing aids 7, 39, 40
 safety of 41–2, 44–7, 50–53
 sulphites 6, 44, 47–8
 thickeners 39, 43, 45, 101
Adult Nutrition Survey 90
Adulteration of food 27–31
Advertising 1, 94–8, 127, 133,
  213–14

to children 94–8, 214
Advertising Standards Authority
82, 89, 132
Aflatoxin 23, 56
Air in food 31, 43, 100
Alar 112, 151
Alcoholic drinks 5, 6, 14, 40, 47–8
alcopops 95
Aldicarb 148
Allergic and intolerant reactions 6,
10–11, 14, 41, 44–5, 90, 101,
108, 116–17, 200
dairy foods 15
peanut allergy 10–11, 117
Allicin 138
Amino acids 87
Anaemia 92
Animal welfare 91, 158, 164–8,
174–9, 206–7
slaughter 168
transport 167
Annatto 22, 36, 44, 48
Anorexia 124
Antibiotics 8, 164, 166, 170,
171–2, 173, 189, 200–201
antibiotic marker genes 196–7,
200–201
Antioxidants 136–7
Appetite 128
suppressants 132
Apple juice
patulin in 56
Apples 147, 151
Artificial sweeteners 20, 39, 45,
49–52, 68, 99, 102, 114–15,
127–8, 133
Ascorbic acid 36
Aspartame (NutraSweet) 45, 50, 52,
68, 128

Babies and children 41, 46,
93–117, 155
Baby foods and drinks 37, 46, 49,
60, 105–14, 109–14, 155
Alar in 112
beef in 11
genetically-altered 111, 205
gluten in 15, 110
herbal drinks 113–14
hydrolysed vegetable protein in
110
maltodextrin in 109, 111, 112, 113
modified starch in 110
organic 111, 112, 205
sugar in 109, 112–14
vitamins and minerals in 110, 112
water in 110
Baby milks see Formula milks
Bacon 4, 29, 30, 33, 69
Beef 11–12, 33, 146
Beer 47–8
Best before dates 4
Beta-carotene see Vitamins and
minerals
Bio-yoghurts 83–4
Bisphenol-A 55
Body Mass Index (BMI) 120
Botulism 25
Bottled water 15–16, 29, 155
Bovine somatotropin (BST) 166,
193, 195–6, 202
Bovine spongiform encephalopathy
see BSE
Box schemes 159, 162
Bran see Fibre
Bread 16, 30, 60, 69, 88, 104
Breakfast cereals 60, 69, 80, 88,
95, 98–9, 104, 105
Breastfeeding 105–6, 108, 116

Breastmilk 55, 62, 106
British Diabetic Association 21
British Medical Association 144,
    152
British Medical Journal 69
Brown FK 36
BSE 11, 146, 158, 164, 166, 181–4,
    187
Bulimia 124
Bulk sweeteners 45, 50, 52, 67

Caffeine 36, 86
Calcium 70, 86, 92, 94, 98, 104
Calcium carbonate 36
Calcium sulphate 37
Calves 167
Cancer 25, 42, 44–5, 47, 49, 50, 54,
    55, 56, 58, 59, 70, 87, 90, 91,
    102, 107, 112, 130, 136, 138,
    140, 144, 151, 154
  breast cancer 143, 148
Cancer Research Campaign 102
Canthaxanthin 23, 44, 46
Carageenan 37, 45
Caramel 16, 37, 44
Carbohydrate 72, 73, 74–5, 127
Carboxylmethylcellulose 37
Carotenoids 129–30, 137
Carrots 147
Celery 147
Cereal bars 99
Charity endorsements 34
Cheese 28, 40, 47, 192, 194
Cheshire Trading Standards 20
Chewing gum 47
Chicken 33, 164–5
  chicken nuggets 30
Chickens see Poultry
Chief Medical Officer 68, 108

Children 79, 85, 93–117, 124, 141,
    152
  and artificial sweeteners 50–52,
    114–15
Chips 94
Chitosan 132
Chlormequat 149
Chocolate 17, 149, 153
Cholesterol 58–9, 71–2, 73, 85, 87
Claims 22–3, 48–9, 158
  dietary supplements 87–9, 139
  extra 5
  fat 63–4, 87
  flavour/flavoured 2
  fresh 23
  general 81
  health 80–89
  light/lite 21, 62, 63–4, 67, 128–9
  low fat 18, 62–4, 87, 128
  medicinal claims 81, 88, 89
  natural 22–3, 48
  nutrition 63, 65–6, 72, 80–81
  organic 158–9
  premium 18–19, 20
  sugar 65–7
  style 23
Clingfilm see Packaging
Cochineal 14, 23
Coeliac disease 14, 110
Coffee 28
Colours see Additives
Committee on Toxicity (COT) 51
Common Agricultural Policy 156
Compassion in World Farming 177
Composition standards 3, 19
Confectionery see Sweets
Conservation Grade 33
Consumers' Association 9, 18, 29,
    57, 90, 170, 185, 188, 204–5, 210

Consumers International 96
Contamination 53–6
Cook-chilled foods 26
Coronary heart disease *see* Heart
  Disease
Coronary Prevention Group 127
Crisps and savoury snacks 94, 96,
  99, 102, 114, 130
Creuzfeldt-Jacob disease (CJD)
  164, 182
Cryptosporidium 154
Cyclamates 45, 50–52, 68

Dairy cows 166
Datemarking 4
DDT 55, 148, 149
Department of Education 95
Department of Health 68, 83, 107,
  108, 170, 186, 188, 206
Dental erosion 66, 100
DHA 62, 106
Diabetic foods 20–21, 50
Dieldrin 149
Diet foods and drinks 125–35
  low-calorie ready meals 127
  meal replacement slimming
    foods 126
  miracle slimming products 132–3
  no-fat foods 129–31
  very-low calorie diets 126
Dietary supplements 81, 87–91,
  138
Dieting 118–35
Dioxins 53, 55
Drinking water *see* Water
Dunn Nutrition Unit 124

E coli *see* Food poisoning
E numbers *see* Additives

Eggs 8, 14, 33, 40, 46, 59, 104, 116,
  164, 177–80, 190
  free-range 158, 178, 179
  organic 158, 179
Elderly 79, 91
Energy 64, 72, 73, 74, 119, 122, 125
Environment 155–6, 158, 172–3,
  198, 201
Environmental Health Officers 211,
  212
Erythrosine 47
European Commission (EC) 12, 63,
  106, 154, 167, 201–2
European Union (EU) 13, 17, 18, 21,
  25, 39, 51, 72, 156, 195

Fairtrade 32, 153, 210
Fast food *see* Takeaway foods
Fat 10, 41, 57, 58–64, 72, 73, 75,
  79, 83, 87, 94, 99, 105, 109,
  122, 126
  busters 132
  cholesterol 58–9, 73
  claims 63–4
  consumption 58
  DHA 62, 106
  'fat-free' fat 53
  hydrogenated 13, 37, 60–61, 99,
    105
  low fat 18, 62–4, 87, 128, 136
  monounsaturates 58, 62, 73
  omega-3 62, 84, 169
  omega-6 61
  polyunsaturates 58, 61, 62, 73
  saturates 58, 59–60, 75, 103, 104,
    105
  substitutes 130–31
  trans fatty acids 59, 60–61
Fertilisers 8, 142, 153–4, 160

Fibre 70–72, 73, 75–6, 79, 83, 85, 87, 98, 99, 104, 127, 136, 149
Fish 28, 43, 62, 84, 194
  farmed 40, 46, 149, 172–3
  fish fingers 3, 100
  fish oils 14, 55, 62, 84, 169
Flavonoids 138
FlavrSavr tomatoes 192, 194–5, 201, 204
Flavour 2, 36
Flavoured 2
Flavourings see Additives
Folic acid 87, 88–9, 138
Follow-on milks 108–9
Food Advisory Committee 46, 82, 115
Food Commission 63, 82, 87, 89, 99, 105, 109, 110, 111, 126, 186, 210
Food and Drink Federation 69, 198
Food law enforcement officers 27
Food miles 160–62
Food poisoning 26, 40, 106, 184–90, 212
  botulism 25
  campylobacter 171, 184, 185, 189
  E coli 163, 168, 184, 186, 187–8
  listeria 26, 188
  salmonella 106, 154, 163, 171, 184, 185, 188–9
Formula milk 46, 53, 55, 62, 105–9, 116, 193
  follow-on milks 108
  soya formula milks 55, 107
Freedom Food 33, 177, 179
Free-range 33, 175, 178, 179
Freezing 25–6, 140
Fresh 19, 23–7, 140, 180
Friends of the Earth 154
Fromage frais 101

Fruit
  chemical treatment of 25, 40, 150–51
  dried 104
  fruit juice 3, 19–20, 29, 100
  gas ripening 27
  tinned 4
  waxed 14, 24, 47
Fruit and vegetables 57, 62, 87, 92, 94, 102, 103, 136–62, 140, 141, 152, 154
Functional foods 81–7
  see also Health claims
Fungicides see Pesticides

Garlic 87, 89
Gas ripening 27
Gelatin 11, 14, 183
Gender-bender chemicals see Oestrogen-mimics
Genetic engineering 8, 111, 124, 139–40, 159, 166, 191–208
Gingko biloba 86
Ginseng 86
Gluten 14–15, 110
Growth hormones/promoters 8, 165, 167, 169–70
Guar gum 37
Guarana 86

Ham 9, 29, 188
Health claims 80–89
Health Education Authority 89
Heart disease 58, 70, 75, 85, 87, 89, 90, 91, 130, 136, 138
Herbicides see Pesticides
High blood pressure 70, 87
Hormones see Growth hormones/promoters

Hydrogenated oils/fat 13, 37, 60–61, 99, 105
Hydrogenation 60
Hydrolysed vegetable protein 13, 37, 110
Hyperactivity 41, 44–5, 101, 116–17
Hypertension *see* High blood pressure

Ice cream 31, 100
Indoles 138
Insecticides *see* Pesticides
Integrated crop management (ICM) 157
Integrated pest management (IPM) 157
Intense sweeteners *see* Artificial sweeteners
Intensive agriculture 155–6, 161
Iron 92, 94, 104, 105, 108
Irradiation 7, 26–7, 29, 159
Isothiocyanates 138, 139
Isotonic *see* Sports drinks

Labelling
  additives 7, 40, 47–8
  alcoholic drinks 47–8
  artificial sweeteners 52, 115
  bottled water 15–16
  bread 16, 26
  cholesterol 59
  datemarking 4
  diabetic foods 20–21
  diet foods 125, 127, 133–5
  eggs 177–9, 180
  fat substitutes 131
  fats 61, 63–4
  fruit juice 19–20

genetically engineered foods 8, 13–14, 198–9, 203–4
  ingredients 4
  irradiated food 26–7
  low alcohol drinks 6, 21, 48
  meat 8, 17–19, 174–7, 186
  mechanically recovered meat (MRM) 12
  microwave ovens 21–2
  modified atmosphere packaging 24–5
  nutrition 5, 9, 60, 72–9, 87
  Olestra 130
  organic food 33, 158–9
  peanuts 10–11, 117
  pesticides 25, 140–41, 150–51
  place of origin 5, 8
  post harvest treatments 25
  production methods 8
  salt 69
  sausages 18
  sugars 65–7, 113
  trans fatty acids 60–61
  vegetarian foods 32
  waxed fruit 24
  weight 4
Lamb 33
Lead 155
Lettuce 148, 153–4
Light *see* Claims
Limonene 138
Lindane 148, 149
Listeria 26
Lite *see* Claims
Litesse 131
Low alcohol drinks 6, 21
Low-calorie ready meals 127
Low fat *see* Claims
Lutein 137

Lycopene 137, 140

Mad cow disease *see* BSE
Maize 13, 193
Maltodextrin 37, 109, 111, 113
Margarine 60–61
Martin Luther King 160
Maximum Residue Level (MRL) 141, 144, 147
McDonald's 95, 96–7
Meal replacement slimming foods 126
Meat 28, 110, 163–90
  frozen 25
  meat alternatives 105
  meat content 5, 7
  meat labelling 8, 11–12, 17–19
  meat, lean 17–18
  mechanically recovered meat (MRM) 12, 43, 181, 189
Mechanically recovered meat (MRM) 12, 43, 181, 189
Medical Research Council 54
Medicines Control Agency 89
Methyl bromide 150
Microwave ovens 21–2, 26, 53, 189
Milk 15, 40, 63, 98, 108, 116, 148, 166, 168–9, 170, 183, 193, 195–6
  formula milk 46, 53, 55, 62, 105–9, 193
  reduced-fat milks 63, 109
Mineral hydrocarbon oils and waxes 47
Mineral water *see* Bottled water
Ministry of Agriculture, Fisheries and Food (MAFF) 21, 47, 51, 56, 63, 78, 107, 112, 143, 144, 145, 147, 154, 160, 173, 181, 183, 188, 202

Mintel 93
Modified atmosphere packaging 24–5
Modified starch 13, 15, 110
Monosodium glutamate 37
Monounsaturated fats 58, 62, 73

National Consumer Council 81, 95
National Food Alliance 132, 214
Natural 22–3, 48, 65
Natural Resources Defense Council 152
Nitrites 49, 153–4
No-fat foods 129–31
NutraSweet *see* Aspartame
Nutrition claims *see* Claims
Nutrition information 5, 8, 9, 60, 72–9, 87
Nutrition Task Force 68
Nuts 56, 62, 104, 200

Oats 71, 87
Obesity 118, 123, 124, 128
Oestrogen-mimics 54–6, 106, 107
Olestra 53, 129–31
Olive oil 28, 62
Omega-3/omega-6 fats *see* Fats
Orange juice *see* Fruit juice
Organic 33, 152, 157, 158–60, 175, 184, 210
  baby food 111, 205
Organochlorine pesticides 55
Organophosphate pesticides 141, 143, 146, 147, 152
Osteoporosis 70, 86, 104, 124
Overweight 118, 123
OXFAM 32

Packaging 1, 31, 53, 55

modified atmosphere packaging 24–5
vacuum packaging 24
Partially hydrogenated vegetable oils *see* Hydrogenated vegetable oil
Paselli 131
Pasta 28
Patulin 56
PCBs 55
Peanuts 10, 56
  allergy 10–11, 117
Pears 149
Pesticides 8, 54, 55, 140–57, 158, 196
  in baby foods 112
  and children 152
  DDT 55, 148, 149
  in drinking water 154, 155
  fish farming 173
  fungicides 24, 25, 142, 148
  herbicides 142
  insecticides 142, 148, 196
  lindane 148
  methyl bromide 150
  organochlorine 55
  organophosphates 141, 143, 146, 147, 152
  poisoning 142–3, 153, 161
Pesticides Action Network 148
Phthalates 53, 55, 107
Phytochemicals 136–8
Phytoestrogens 55, 107–8
Pigs 165–6
Polyphosphate additives 29
Polyunsaturated fats 58, 61, 62, 73
Pork 33, 165–6
  outdoor reared 165, 176
Potatoes 25, 148, 150

Poultry 46, 176, 185
  see also Chicken
Prawns 30
Premium *see* Claims
Preservatives *see* Additives
Prickly ash bark 86
Processed food 27, 40, 41, 42, 60, 69, 102, 103, 122, 127, 129, 193
Processing aids *see* additives
Protein 72, 73, 74, 83, 98, 104, 126

Quantitative ingredient declarations (QUID) 3

Real Meat Company 175
Restaurant food 6, 27
Rice 28
Royal Society for the Protection of Birds (RSPB) 156, 177
RSPCA 33

Saccharin 45, 50, 68, 115, 128
Salatrim 131
Salmonella *see* Food poisoning
Salt 41, 57, 68–70, 72, 73, 76, 79, 87, 98, 102, 127
Salt substitutes 70
Saturated fats 58, 59–60, 72, 73, 75, 103, 104, 105
Sausages 18–19, 29, 43, 69, 94
Scampi 28, 29
Schizandra 86
Schools 95
Scrapie 164
Selenium 137, 138
Sheep 167
  sheep dips 143, 146
Shellac 38
Shropshire Trading Standards 103

Simplesse 130
Slendid 131
Slimmers 64, 76, 104
Slimming 118–35
  pills 132
Sodium *see* Salt
Soft drinks 10, 34, 36, 49, 67, 86,
    87, 94, 96, 100–101, 112–14, 127
  'diet' drinks 49, 100
  juice drinks 20
  sports drinks 85–6
  'squash drinking syndrome' 114
  sugar-free 66, 100
Soil Association 33, 159, 162, 184
Soup 7
Soya 13, 55, 105, 111, 116, 197–9,
    204
  soya formula milks 55, 107
Spices 29
Spina bifida 87, 88
Spinach 153–4
Sponsorship 95
Sports drinks 85–6
Sports endorsements 34
Spring water *see* Bottled water
Strawberries 150
Sugar 10, 41, 57, 64–7, 72, 73, 74–5,
    79, 83, 86, 94, 98, 99, 100 101,
    102, 108, 114, 115, 126, 128
  alternatives 67–8
  in baby foods 109
  claims 65–7
  content of foods 67
  extrinsic sugars 64–5, 75
  intrinsic sugars 64, 75
Sulphites 6, 44, 47–8
Supermarkets 27, 32, 34, 80, 145,
    150, 153, 157, 159, 204–5, 210,
    215–16

Sweets 40, 47, 87, 94, 96, 101
  tooth-friendly 34, 101

Take away foods 6, 40, 60, 61, 69
Tartrazine 38, 48
Taurine 86
Tecnazene 25
Thaumatin 68
Tooth decay 64, 79, 100–101, 108,
    109, 113, 114
Tooth-friendly sweets 34, 50
Trading Standards 211, 212
Trans fatty acids 59, 60–61
Tuna, tinned 4
Turkeys 25–6, 165

United Kingdom Register of
    Organic Food Standards
    (UKROFS) 158
Unwrapped foods 6
Use by dates 4

Vacuum packaging 24
Vanilla 28
Veal 167
Vegans 14, 24, 91–2, 104–5
Vegetable oil 28
Vegetables *see* Fruit and vegetables
Vegetarian 14, 32, 91–2, 103–5,
    130, 163, 206
Vegetarian food 60, 105
Vegetarian Society 32, 103
Very-low calorie diets 126
Vitamins and minerals 73, 83, 85,
    87, 94, 98, 101, 102, 110, 126,
    127, 129, 138, 160
  beta-carotene 90, 139
  calcium 86, 92, 94, 98, 104
  carotenoids 129–30, 137, 139

folic acid 87, 88–9, 138
and IQ 103
iron 92, 94, 104, 105, 108
selenium 137, 138
vitamin A 90, 129–30, 137, 170
vitamin B_6 90
vitamin B_{12} 92, 105
vitamin C 20, 102, 104, 112,
   137–8, 140
vitamin D 129–30
vitamin E 129–30, 137, 138
vitamin K 129–30
see also Dietary supplements

Water 54, 55, 114, 154–5
   bottled 15–16, 155
   in food 5, 9, 29–30, 43, 110
Waxes 14, 24
Weight 4
Whisky 28
Wine 28, 40, 48
World Health Organization 106,
      108, 115, 142, 143, 155, 171

Yoghurt 29, 101, 161
   bio-yoghurts 83–4